Banking on Angels

How an Investment Banker Found Spiritual
Fulfillment and Inner Peace

Neal Bakshi

BANKING ON ANGELS

HOW AN INVESTMENT BANKER FOUND SPIRITUAL
FULFILLMENT AND INNER PEACE

Neal Bakshi

For more information:

Email: neal@nealbakshi.com

Website: https://www.nealbakshi.com

Instagram: @neal.bakshi

ISBN: 979-8-9874559-4-4

Free Angel Gifts

For more resources, workbooks, guides, and references like those found in this book, visit
https://www.nealbakshi.com/bankingonangels
or scan the below QR code!

This book is dedicated to my mom and guardian angel, Simi Bakshi. I'm grateful for her endless support, guidance, and love. She has made me into the person I am today and showers me with blessings on my life path from the Other Side.

Table of Contents

Introduction

Thank you for picking up this book and being here right now! Whatever timely event led you to this book happened for a very meaningful reason.

I'm Neal Bakshi, and I'm a spiritual life coach, reiki energy healer, and soul-centered entrepreneur.

I specialize in helping highly driven and motivated next-gen leaders in their fields achieve higher vibrational energetic states and emotional balance. Through personal practice of meditation for over twenty-five years, I infuse spiritual modalities such as meditation, breathwork, and energy clearing into my programs. I help changemakers cultivate deep inner peace, co-create their abundant personal reality, open their eyes to new perspectives, and leave a meaningful and lasting legacy in the world.

I grew up in Princeton, New Jersey, and had the blessing of being born into a spiritual family. I was raised following the spiritual path of Self-Realization Fellowship (SRF) founded by Paramahansa Yogananda in 1920. As such, I started learning scientific methods of yogic meditation since I was five years old.

I graduated from New York University (NYU) with a bachelor's in economics and history. I spent the next eight years working on Wall Street in investment banking, leaving Goldman Sachs as a vice president in 2022.

While most investment bankers dislike their roles due to the long hours and incessant work, I largely enjoyed what I did. The work was fast paced, the people were awesome, I could handle my own, and I got paid well. Sure, there were some drawbacks, but that's part of the natural duality of life.

I grew up wanting nothing more than to be an investment banker. In fact, when I was twelve years old, my seventh-grade teacher asked our class to work on a project of what we each wanted to be when we grew up. We were supposed to write an essay on the topic and make business cards for ourselves as part of the assignment. I remember sitting behind a colorful Apple iMac that resembled a rounded pyramid placed on its side. In the Word document, I typed my name, title, home address, AOL email, and in big, bold, capital, and italicized letters wrote my firm's name—Bakshi Bucks—on my future business card. You could genuinely say I was manifesting my future reality from the time I was in middle school.

You're probably asking yourself how a twelve-year-old knows so adamantly that they want to be an investment banker. Growing up, I had a mom who worked in healthcare finance, and I was always drawn to the money side of the things she did.

Additionally, every year we would go to a big Christmas party with all my parents' good friends and their families. In Indian culture, this was essentially like extended family. Most of the men ("uncles") I was surrounded by at these family gatherings were high-flying hedge fund managers, tenured investment banking Managing Directors (MDs), Merger & Acquisition (M&A) deal closers, and sales traders. Their houses were awe-inspiring, their cars were trendy, their spirits seemed jolly, and their lives appeared safe and extraordinarily comfortable. If working in finance and making millions of dollars could provide all of this—I wanted nothing more.

However, when the person who loved me more than I loved myself suddenly disappeared from the face of this Earth, everything changed.

In June 2020, my mom went in for what was supposed to be a routine procedure—a thirty-minute outpatient thumb surgery to fix a partially torn ligament. Under anesthesia, she suffered an arrest and couldn't be roused after the surgery. She spent nearly three weeks in the ICU on life support, and ultimately passed on.

Over the following months, this grave scenario revealed just how out-of-balance my life was—even when I thought everything was perfect. I was overly focusing on the material personal gain I would stand to earn as a banker, neglecting my own personal, emotional, and spiritual growth along the way. Given that all of these aspects of life consume and expend energy, I eventually boiled it down to being out of balance *energetically*.

After my mom's passing, I spent the first six months picking up the pieces for myself and my family. The following six months in early 2021, I started to tune in to signs from the Universe—in meditation, through numbers, suddenly meeting new people, and so on.

As I explain in more detail later on, there was an invisible force leading me to help people. As a result, I got certified in life coaching and started my own coaching business. Clients came in almost immediately and saw profoundly meaningful change in their lives, from job changes to new relationships. Coaching felt natural, it lit me up, and people seemed to find me through the most interesting ways when they needed me most.

Through the certifications and accreditations, I've garnered the framework with which to help guide high achievers to reach their goals and find personal balance. Yet even more powerfully, through my own personal journey and firsthand experience, I've come to realize new and profoundly life-changing perspectives for my greatest benefit. It has allowed me to intertwine energy tools, intuition, meditation, science, spirituality, and positive psychology to unleash a holistic and multi-dimensional approach to my personal growth.

While the surface-level symptoms may differ from person to person, the common denominator among all people is energy.

Once I started experimenting to see how I could interact, feel, move, direct, and rely on energy, I started to build a well of faith and belief within myself. This went to show me that energy work was actually real and was yielding genuine results over months of tangible practice.

It started with scientific methods of meditation, breathwork, and *pranayama* (life-force control). Coupled with brain-rewiring visualization and journaling techniques, I started to see my business grow, self-confidence improve, self-belief kick into high gear, and clients manifest per my exact request.

As the months went on, I realized it was my mom—one of my guardian angels—nudging me along this newfound path I was supposed to take. I began to cultivate a dialogue with her, the angelic realm (my spirit guides), and the broader Universe. This opened up entirely new avenues of neurological perception I never even knew existed.

From there, I was guided into learning about deeper spiritual concepts and plant medicines, like ayahuasca, from indigenous shamans in the Peruvian Amazon. I learned Japanese reiki energy healing; went on spiritual pilgrimages through Egypt, Jordan, and Israel; attended Temescal sweat lodges and breathwork certifications in Ibiza; cultivated and practiced my channeling abilities; and undertook countless other spiritual studies and ceremonies around the world. All of this allowed me to realize and feel the common thread underlying all cultures and traditions as it relates to the world of energy.

Learning was just the first step. Daily practice on myself and others proved to me that the unseen world of energy carries far more influence than we think. I tuned in, devoted myself, asked for guidance, surrendered into the flow, and found all that I was looking for and more.

Today, I feel calmer and more present than ever before. I am able to detach from the incessant identification with my thoughts and emotions, and view them from the perspective of my higher mind. I feel less triggered by external situations outside of my control and have a deep sense of peace and trust in the path my life has and is taking me on.

On a daily basis, I work on increasing my self-awareness and turning down the external distractions. As a result, I have learned how to tap into deep meditative states to receive intuitive guidance and channeled messages.

Through personal experimentation, I created an almost-too-simple approach to opening my heart, releasing egoic identification, and finding emotional clarity. This practice has allowed me to reprogram my subconscious mind for intrinsic self-belief, slow down to notice the magic of synchronicity happening all around me, and most remarkably, allow me to physically manifest my reality. Through consistency, the results compound daily and have become engrained as habits that allow for a fast track in my own physical, emotional, mental, and spiritual energetic development.

I've been able to achieve all of this, and I know it's possible for you as well. It is undeniably a *journey* and one that must be taken with intention. The end destination is 1 percent of the entire process. It's about the 99 percent lead-up that you must be all-in for. The experiences, setbacks, breakthroughs, learnings, and integration that occurs along the way is where the growth is truly felt. It's when you look back once you've reached the destination (or a better one!) and are in awe of the person you are and all you have been through to get to that point.

In my post-banking day-to-day work, I now help CFOs, startup founders, entrepreneurs, biotech executives, and hard-running financiers create their dream lives. It all starts on the inside and radiates outward. We're spiritual, energetic beings living a human existence in a material world. Tapping into the energy behind your reality and understanding practical spiritual truths unleashes dormant potential energy. Cultivating this energetic balance and vibrational uplift is the key to your lasting and recurring personal success and global impact.

In the pages that follow, you'll embark on a scientific, spiritual, and psychological personal growth journey. Through my own story as a vice president in investment banking at Goldman Sachs, you'll get a glimpse into my former banker life and see some of my symptoms of energetic imbalance.

In the remainder of this introduction, you'll learn about the various energy bodies and how quantum physics can help you understand that everything is simply energy in constant vibration. You'll learn about what the problem of energetic imbalance really is, how to tune in with that, and how to effectuate change in your own life.

In Part 1, I'll share tangible coaching frameworks and practical steps you can take to generate greater degrees of self awareness, remove distractions, balance your energy, and dive deep into your own experimentation with personal growth. This is the beginning of your journey to inner peace.

My story of connecting with my angels and asking the Universe for guidance is a big part of why I'm so calm, peaceful, and trusting of what unfolds around me. I'll share my personal story with you and how I started to cultivate this dialogue with the Universe and my spirit guides. Whether or not you share my beliefs or perspective is completely fine. All I ask is that you remain open and see what resonates most with you. Later on, I'll even give you a sneak peek into how to call upon your angels for guidance and support in any life situation you face. Try it for yourself and see what differences you notice in your life.

In Part 2, I'll share the tangible Five Pillars of Greater Fulfillment I don't start a day without. After years of experimentation, I boiled down a personal and spiritual growth practice to a five-minute single-page daily journal entry. I break each one down and, most importantly, explain *why* they work. You can download a free journal to get you started on this practice at my website, https://www.nealbakshi.com/bankingonangels.

Last, in Part 3, I'll leave you with closing thoughts about how you can continue living your life in a balanced energetic way. By the end, you'll have the tools and awareness to choose an elevated vibrational state every day.

Why does energetic vibration and balance matter?

It's how you achieve inner peace and new perspective. It's where things like a loved one dying becomes not the end of a relationship but rather the growth of your ability to communicate beyond words.

It's how you can slow down to tap into the energy swirling all around you. In doing so, you can consciously co-create your dream life (or something better).

It's where you're able to get real with yourself, rewire beliefs from childhood, and fast-track your personal life and professional goals.

I wrote this book for my fellow corporate hustlers working in investment banking and other fast-paced, busy, and high-pressure roles across the world. If you're a self-starter, someone who's committed to creating the best possible life for themselves and their loved ones, and ready to see how you can unlock greater fulfillment in your life starting today, this book is for you.

Over the past few years, I've come to realize that nothing happens by chance. It's not a coincidence you picked up this book.

It's not a random occurrence you're reading these specific words. Every little action, interaction, thought, word, emotion, situation, and choice you've made since birth has coalesced to lead you to this very moment.

If you proceed with your own conscious intention and continually come back to that intention along the way, you'll notice a shift within yourself. It may not be all at once, but the effects will slowly build. Like a snowball rolling down a hill, it will take shape, gather speed, and grow.

Pause for a minute and think about what your intention in reading this book is. Maybe it's how to find greater balance in your life, learn about the science behind mindfulness, expand your spiritual understanding, learn tools and techniques you can implement in your daily life, or even just hear my story as a former Goldman Sachs VP who communicates with angels.

The journey is about finding your way to be here now. Most of all, it's about having fun and learning in the physical world while simultaneously nourishing your spiritual needs. Whatever your intention is, think of it now.

This intention will help direct your energy to receive the most from this book. When you feel drained, exhausted, or unmotivated—come back to that intention. That is when you need it most, and that will help you regain your footing to find your energetic balance.

When you're done with this book, email me at neal@nealbakshi. com. This book was written with the energy of helping you realize the power that lies within your own spirituality and self-belief. Share with me your biggest takeaway, and see how that act of consciously pausing and reflecting creates benevolent ripple effects in your life. As Harvard researcher turned spiritual teacher, Richard Alpert (also known as Ram Dass) said, "We're all just walking each other home."[1]

Everything Is Energy

"Everything is energy and that's all there is to it. Match the frequency of the reality you want and you cannot help but get that reality. It can be no other way. This is not philosophy. This is physics."

—Albert Einstein, Theoretical Physicist

It was the sunny summer morning of our 2019 annual group golf outing at Goldman Sachs. However, instead of being in a car from Manhattan to Long Island, I found myself in the back seat of an Uber driving me home four blocks from the gym.

That morning, I experienced the most intense flare-up yet of two herniated discs in my lower back—a condition I had as a result of a weightlifting injury seven years prior. I went to see multiple doctors and imaging specialists on a same-day emergency basis. The diagnosis from the X-rays and MRIs: I would undoubtedly need spine surgery within my lifetime.

For over a week, I was unable to move off the floor. Stabbing back pain at the age of twenty-seven, like a knife driven into me with every slight movement. Little did I know that long before I would be introduced to the world of energy healing, I unknowingly healed my chronic lower back pain in a matter of months.

I was petrified when I got the spine surgery diagnosis, but a good friend recommended I read the book *Healing Back Pain* by Dr. John Sarno. In his best-selling book, Dr. Sarno, a professor and doctor at NYU, shared numerous case studies and findings from working with rehabilitation patients over decades. He found that lower back pain is principally the result of what he calls Tension Myoneural Syndrome (TMS). His belief from examining hundreds of patients was that TMS is caused by repressed emotions (primarily anger) held in the body. At the end of the book, he shares twelve steps and affirmations for overcoming the issue.

I was skeptical to say the least, but I was completely immobile, taking muscle relaxers that left me in a daze, and sleeping on the floor; I was willing to try anything. As weeks went on, I practiced what he laid out in his book. Dr. Sarno's protégé didn't have any appointments for over two months, but by the time the appointment came around, I had weaned off all medications and found that I was nearly completely healed from an injury that had plagued me all through my twenties. The wildest part was that there was nearly no medical intervention after I made up my mind to follow Dr. Sarno's psychological healing protocol.

Modern medicine is a phenomenal gift we're lucky to enjoy in our current day and age. I've also learned that it's only part of the equation and can be amplified with other techniques in your ability. Meditation, visualization, and affirmative thought are amazing things to talk about in theory, but how do they actually work?

The answer is surprisingly simple: energy.

Research from twentieth-century Noble Prize laureates proves the scientific basis that *everything* in our known universe is made of energy. This same scientific basis is the proof behind metaphysical truths such as meditation and energy healing.

As humans, we're conditioned to believe it when we see it. Seeing energy through the lens of the world's greatest scientists builds belief in why spiritual practices work. From this perspective, the techniques in this book will have an even stronger impact on your overall quality of life—and can even heal your physical body.

Albert Einstein developed the theories of relativity and quantum physics we use to this day. If everything is energy, this means that beyond just your physical body, your emotions, thoughts, and spiritual "gut feelings" are also energy.

Energy is usually regarded as the capacity for doing work.[2] It can be transformed or transferred from one form to another, but cannot be created or destroyed.[3] As such, the total amount of energy in the universe is constant.

Energy can take any number of forms and is all around you. A campfire, the lights in your house, going for a walk, speaking, turning a doorknob, and fruit falling from a tree are all examples.

Think about when you walk into a room or meet someone new. You can immediately feel if the energy (or the "vibe"—short for vibration) is inviting or "off." You can feel the energetic vibration at a big concert, wedding, or even walking down the streets of New York City. Similarly, you can feel calming energy when you're relaxing on a beach, unwinding by a campfire, or spending a day at the spa.

On the smallest level, we're energetically made of constantly vibrating electrons (electricity) and photons (light). In fact, there are numerous instances to show how through attention and concentration on energetic frequencies, you can actually effect change in your physical, mental, and emotional states of well-being on this subatomic level.

Another good example of how energy can heal and change the physical body has been explained by Vishen Lakhiani, the founder of personal growth platform Mindvalley. He famously recalls his story about how he miraculously healed his five-year stint with severe acne through meditative visualization techniques in just five weeks.[4]

The Science of Vibration

To understand how the frequency of your thoughts can affect the vibration of your body, you need go a little bit deeper into the science behind quantum physics. *Quantum* essentially means the behavior of matter and energy on the subatomic (unseen) level.

Here, we find that mass is just a manifestation of energy. This means that everything, including the human body you find yourself in, is simply energy stored in solid form.

Wave-particle duality and quantum wave theory state that the light and electricity we're made of can behave as particles as well as waves.[5] So, what does this really mean?

According to Sir Isaac Newton, a physicist from the late 1600s, photons and electrons appear as singular packets of energy known as particles. These particles aggregate together to create the physical world we see at any given moment. Think of it like a puzzle. A single piece is a particle, and the entire completed puzzle is all the particles put together to create a full picture.

In 1927, German physicist Werner Heisenberg demonstrated that photons and electrons can also take the form of waves (or fields). These quantum fields don't sit still and can take a value at *any* point in space. They are moving, vibrating, and changing in value over time, much like the waves of an ocean.

For example, think about being at a concert. The sound you hear at any point within the venue would have a value. That value would be louder in the front of the concert hall (by the speakers) and quieter in the back. This would be a field of sound.

Another example is the heat you feel sitting at varying distances around a campfire: hotter near the fire and cooler away from it. This is a thermodynamic field.

What we see around us can be boiled down to the movement of light and the vibration of electricity in their respective fields. A basic visualization of fields can be shown by putting a magnet together with some metal filings; the pattern the metal filings create is analogous to the magnet's unseen magnetic field.

Without going too deep down the rabbit hole of Quantum Field Theory (QFT), you can also see this happen when you call someone on your cell phone. As the phone rings, you are putting excitations into the electromagnetic field that is broadcasting from you to the cell tower and onto the field of the person you are calling.

Erwin Schrödinger won the Nobel Prize in physics in 1933 for his famed Schrödinger's equation. This was a crucial discovery, helping to explain that when you observe a field, you are actually only observing a particle at a specific location.

The fields, like the waves of the open ocean, are constantly vibrating and moving. But when measured, they collapse into a singular position of where that particle is in that field at that instance. In our example, it would be how high that wave was when we measured it.

The quantum field itself is consistently moving and behaves differently when not actively observed. Understanding QFT, you can begin to see how *everything* is energy in constant vibration.

Take a closer look at the physical construct of your body to really grasp this and see how you can use energy to expedite healing it. Examining the skin, the largest organ in your body, shows that this tissue is created of superimposed fields—one on top of another.[6]

Look at your hand. At first, you notice the wrinkles and small hairs. You can feel the solid texture of anything around you as you touch it. Magnified 20,000 times under a microscope, the solid mass of skin turns into a field of undulating cells.

Even greater magnification shows the organelles inside the cells, and still greater magnification shows the particles within subatomic energy fields that comprise those organelles. With vast distances between each spinning electron, zooming in reveals that on the subatomic level, the skin is 99.99999% empty space.[7]

Taking what we know from our QFT lesson, we see that these particles are just units of energy within a vast field. Therefore, while the skin tissue appears solid, in particle form, it is actually superimposed dynamic energy in constant movement and vibration. Take a second to let that sink in.

Seeing yourself on the quantum level of energy is a wakeup call to the magnitude of power you have to effectuate change in your life from the smallest scale to the biggest picture, from the inside out. When you walk into a 3-D movie, you put on 3-D glasses to get the full experience. As you go through this book, put on your energy glasses to get the most from this experience.

With these glasses, you realize *you* are pure energy with the potential to move and change energy. From that perspective, the practical tools and techniques I share in Part 2 onward take a foothold rooted in the accepted scientific reality of our physical existence.

When you can see past the physical symptoms into the energy symptoms, you can put practices in place with conscious intention to balance the energy across your life, find inner peace, and flow.

The Four Core Energetic Bodies

There are various schools of thought on just how many energy bodies we're made of. Through my spiritual upbringing, life coaching practice, and energy healing learnings, I can currently simplify it down to four of the easiest to understand. They are the Physical, Emotional, Mental, and Spiritual. A simple acronym to remember this is PEMS.

Jill Willard is a gifted intuitive and meditation instructor. She is also the author of the book *Intuitive Being*. In her various works, Jill similarly conveys the importance of balance across all four energetic bodies.[8] This balance allows you to feel less fatigued, more grounded, and experience greater vitality, longevity, and health.

The physical body is just as you'd expect. It's your skin, brain, organs, and everything comprising what you see when you look in the mirror. It's also the physical stuff inside you: every part of the skeletal system, blood, veins, muscles, and tissues underneath. This body of energy is highly intelligent—more so than we give it credit for. It gives us near-immediate biofeedback as to what makes it feel good, what hurts it, heals it, and allows it to grow to feel fully vibrant and in its power.

Your physical body naturally contains what's called a proprioceptive system. This is your body's ability to sense movement, action, and location. It's also known as kinesthesia and is located in your muscles and joints. It provides you with a sense of bodily and spatial awareness.[9] Without it, you wouldn't be able to move without thinking about your next step or touch your elbow with your eyes closed.

This bodily system senses inputs and determines how you respond to sensory stimuli. It feeds into your peripersonal space and your emotional energetic body. Your peripersonal space, as defined by psychiatrists and behavioral neuroscientists, is the space surrounding your body where you can reach or be reached by objects or other people. This allows you to protect your body while simultaneously interacting with the world around you.[10] Karla McLaren, M.Ed is an award-winning author and social science researcher based in California. She explains the peripersonal boundary as an eighteen-to-thirty-inch oval around you in all directions.[11] In spiritual terms, you can consider this your aura.

Your emotional body is where your worldly experiences are felt, synthesized, and start the interpretation process. It's related to your nervous system, hormones, and water release/absorption (tears/bloating). The emotional body often wants to dictate how you react, make sense of, and respond to circumstances and outside energies.

In balance, the emotional body is empathic, honest, inclusive, and non-judgmental. It also allows the hormones and systems that govern the physical body to operate optimally for your overall health and well-being (i.e., blood pressure, cortisol, and heart rate).

Think about an instance where you experienced heartbreak. Maybe a breakup, rejection, or loss of a loved one. You likely felt this heartbreak very deeply emotionally. Maybe you cried, sat on the couch watching movies and eating a pint of Ben & Jerry's ice cream, or couldn't get out of bed or stop thinking about this person. This is an example of an over-balanced emotional body. Your nervous system was triggered, the hormones in your body caused you to cry, and your physical and mental health may have taken some time to rebalance themselves. Just as the physical body uses energy when you go for a run, the emotional body is constantly using energy as you hop from one experience to another in your day-to-day life situation.

Dr. David R. Hawkins, MD, PhD, is a nationally renowned psychiatrist, physician, researcher, and spiritual teacher. He created a way to test the sound, light, and electromagnetic waves (frequency) coming off the human heart when someone is thinking, emoting, or creating. From this data, he created a logarithmic scale (from 0 to 1,000) called the Hawkins Scale of Consciousness, furthering the science of kinesiology. While not always directly correlated to the emotion itself, the scale ranges from lower vibration states such as shame (20), guilt (30), apathy (50), and grief (75), up to the highest states of love (500), joy (540), peace (600), and enlightenment (700–1,000). When I refer to the energetic vibration of emotions/states of being, I generally like to align it with Hawkins's view that more elevated states of being (through emotions, words, thoughts, actions) result in higher frequencies recorded in your personal attractor (morphogenic) field.

Map of Consciousness Levels

from Dr. David R. Hawkins

700 - 1000	Enlightenment	• Powerful inspiration • Attractor energy fields influence all of humanity
600	Peace	• Transcendence. Oneness with all • Great contributions to the world
540	Joy	• Impact / Effortless / Synchronicity • Individual will merges into Divine will
500 Dissolves Negativity	Love	• Heart-centered motive • True happiness & intuition
400	Reason	• Intelligence & rationality • Knowledge & education
350	Acceptance	• Major transformation • You are the source & creator of life
310	Willingness	• Success, rapid growth • Overcoming inner resistance to life
250	Neutrality	• Energy becomes very positive • Inner confidence
200 Inflection Point	Courage	• Level of Empowerment / Life is exciting
175	Pride	• External Validation
150	Anger	• Hate / Aggression
125	Desire	• Greed / Insatiable
100	Fear	• Worry / Anxiety
75	Grief	• Sadness / Regret & Depression
50	Apathy	• Helplessness / Hopelessness
30	Guilt	• Victimhood / Blame
20	Shame	• Miserable / Humiliation

Note: A person may operate on one level in any given area of life. An individual's overall level of consciousness is the sum total of all levels.

The next energy body is the mental body. As it sounds, it's the home of all your thoughts, attitudes, judgments, and expectations. To a certain degree the mental body (along with your emotional body) also includes your attachments and material desires. The mental body is where intellectual and analytical thought helps you to process information, learn, speak, concentrate, and make logical conclusions.

From my experience working with highly driven individuals, this is often the most over-balanced body. Bankers, lawyers, doctors, C-suite executives, and startup founders are often too frequently in overdrive, given the demanding nature of their worldly roles. This go-go-go, always-on mentality can result in overstimulation and overbalance of mental energetic states relative to the other energy bodies. Oftentimes, the symptoms appear as overthinking, anxiety, irritability, and intense stress or overwhelm.

Last, but of equal emphasis and importance, is the spiritual body. This body is your etheric connection to yourself and everything around you. It is the ability to connect into the broader intelligence and design of the Universe. Here, extreme presence leads to serendipitous moments and intuitive guidance. It's the "gut feeling" telling you to put your foot on the break as a crossing car runs a red light. It's the part of you who thinks about a friend you haven't spoken to in months moments before receiving a call or text from them.

As Jill Willard explains, most people don't acknowledge or understand this aspect exists. Even growing up in a spiritual family, I didn't truly know what this energy could do for me. As such, I downplayed the importance it had in my daily life. Spirituality has little to do with what you believe culturally when it comes to religion or spirits. Rather, it is the understanding that all is one and no one stands alone in this journey of life. [12] While we all have differing life situations and are fighting battles no one knows anything about, the underlying themes and lessons aggregate to a few handfuls of commonly experienced human beliefs.

Everyone has spiritual experiences. Some call it by different names, but what I noticed from coaching is that almost no one has a place to talk about them openly. So many people I come in contact with are suppressing that side of themselves. That suppression leads to spiritual underbalance, and oftentimes, manifests as physical illness or pain.

From doctors to teachers, when my clients were given the opportunity to uncover, freely express, and cultivate their spiritual goals and experiences in a safe space with me, they stepped into a completely new power. In doing so, they were finding ways to move around their high-pressure world with greater confidence and self-trust.

Spirituality also reminds you that we are all fundamentally connected. Life is a mirror, and through helping others, you are also helping yourself. We are all unified through the same life-force, which allows our hearts to beat and lungs to breathe involuntarily.

In fact, the word spirituality derives from the Latin word *spirare*, which means to breathe, to blow, and to live.[13] Spirituality is the breath of life itself—which makes sense if you think about why so many meditation techniques tell you to focus on your breathing.

Meditation is a hot topic in today's world. It is also closely intertwined with the spiritual energetic body. The act of meditation is an opportunity to go within. Feeling this energetic vibration within yourself is the cornerstone to achieving deep states of peace, clarity, and physical healing. This is because your spirit or soul is within the body, animates it, and allows you to then use that energy beyond yourself.

In this self-reflective state of inner silence, you can slow down and open new faculties of the mind. Those faculties allow you to mysteriously accomplish more in less time by unlocking flow states of focused attention and creativity. Meditation is one of the least emphasized actions in our outwardly focused day but provides some of the greatest benefits we are yet to fully comprehend.

Coming into balance across all four of these energetic bodies brings holistic wellness into your life. It removes physical toxins, stress, emotional reactivity, and incessant thought loops. It allows you to solve problems, communicate honestly, and build deeper relationships. It brings a feeling of pervading peace and intrinsic trust and guidance into your life. Utilizing scientific and proven techniques of energy awareness with consistency, you can consciously work with the energy frequencies and fields in your life to create your desired reality.

However, most people walk through life completely unaware that the pain they feel and struggles they experience are due to an energetic imbalance across their four bodies. They typically seek the answers and solutions outside of themselves. Materially, maybe it's the next job promotion, salary raise, house, or car. Maybe it's the next healer, therapist, or online course. Now I'm not saying modern medicine or the very real physical circumstances we come in contact with are not real or true. They very much are and play a vital role in our health, growth, and welfare. Yet the physical solutions are just part of the equation. When combined with the energy tools available to all of us, we unlock greater power and a more determined, disciplined, and resilient mindset. Again, it comes back to balance—both internally and externally.

I came to an interesting realization from the clients I've worked with in my life coaching practice, and from being surrounded by highly aspirational individuals through college and corporate life. The very common theme regardless of which high-pressure, high-stress, time-demanding job you have is that if there is friction or dis-ease, there is typically a form of underlying energetic imbalance in your life. This causes your interconnected Wheel of Life to feel lacking or weighed down in some area.

Energetic Imbalance
Isn't So Obvious

"The wound is the place where the Light enters you."
— Rumi, thirteenth-century Persian poet

For my first four and a half years at Goldman Sachs, I worked on the Leveraged Finance (Lev Fin) Capital Markets & Syndicate desk. My role was one where I would evaluate the credit quality of highly leveraged (below-investment-grade) companies and structure, negotiate, launch, and sell billions of dollars' worth of debt in the form of high-yield bonds and leveraged loans for leveraged buyouts (LBOs), mergers & acquisitions (M&A), refinancings, and other general corporate purposes.

I woke up at 4:30 a.m. to fit in my daily workout, and would hit the desk between 6:30 and 7 a.m. I had to closely follow what was happening with the world's financial markets. My Bloomberg terminal was constantly humming in the background, feeding me data as I would go about my daily tasks. The days were wildly fast paced as I monitored the ever-changing investor sentiment that reacted to economic or political news.

I spent my days compiling market updates, talking to investors, C-suite executives, bond and loan traders, salespeople, and our coverage banking teams. Sitting in investment banking, my job was to bridge the gap between the private side, where deal information is not yet announced, and the public side, where we would sell our deals to investors. We would commit the firm's capital as part of these multibillion-dollar transactions, so we needed to be disciplined and highly calculated in our judgments. Anything that went awry would be our responsibility as the ones managing the firm's risk. Alertness, discipline, and confidence were all necessary. During my time on the desk, I worked on, structured, and sold over $100 billion dollars of high-yield bonds and leveraged loans to hundreds of Wall Street's most reputable asset managers, insurance companies, and hedge funds.

Yet as the years wore on, it became increasingly apparent that I was one of the surprising few in investment banking who enjoyed my job. When the time came to hang up my suit after eight years on Wall Street, I looked back to see that I was the last one left in my group's analyst class.

My job made me feel like I was living the life of a Wall Street banker out of a movie—a life I'd always dreamed of—but it was certainly incessant work. Sixty-hour weeks were often the bare minimum, but most wound up in the eighty-to-one-hundred-hour window.

For eight years, life revolved around one thing—work. Deadlines for everything were to be met "ASAP," "urgently," and "done yesterday." Dinners and dates were regularly canceled because of last-minute overnight projects. Most personal train rides or car trips were spent logged on using my mobile hotspot to send slide decks or Excel files.

I took calls from anywhere at any time imaginable. I woke up at odd hours of the night to post documents to data rooms. Weekends were spent in the office revising version 113 of our quarterly market update. Some nights would be reserved for receiving nonstop emails from the London or Australia teams, asking for work to be done immediately (and following up within minutes if it wasn't).

Working in investment banking, time was not my own. By the end of my nearly decade-long stint on Wall Street, every time I would receive a work email notification on my phone, I would immediately feel a jolt of adrenaline mixed with anxiety and stress creep up my body. What would it say? Would it be directed at me? If it was on Saturday, would I need to stop what I was doing, run home, and log on? If I didn't respond to the MD or partner instantly, how would it reflect on me?

However, I knew what I was signing up for. There's a reason investment banking has a reputation for being grueling, tiring, and intense. Vacations were strategically taken or not taken at all. I remember one planned trip was completely canceled because of a last-minute deal—the four-billion-dollar LBO of the Ultimate Fighting Championship. After all, could you really take a vacation if you were at risk of being viewed as a slacker, missing out on a promotion, or not having the necessary face time with bosses who would decide your fate come bonus season?

When I got to Goldman Sachs, I knew I had to keep my foot on the gas pedal. I distinctly remember one morning as an analyst; I overheard two MDs talking about a layoff the day before. One was talking about how he just fired his associate. He said something along the lines of, "You need to walk into work every day like you're about to get hit by a bus. If you're not coming in with that kind of an attitude, you are replaceable, and someone else will easily take your job."

At the time I heard that, I felt like a Loony Tunes cartoon character with my eyes popping out of my head. The message I took away was crystal clear. I needed to keep my head down, grind it out, perfect my craft, climb the corporate ladder, and make my way to the top of the firm. I was determined to embody the vision of success I had cultivated for myself since childhood, and nothing would get in my way.

I devoted everything to this success and squeezed productivity out of every moment. I didn't waste a minute of my day. I had my entire schedule down to a science and mapped out what I needed to do to get ahead in every part of my life. I was caught in a productivity trap. A busy trap. A chase to the top of the corporate ladder where all of my happiness would be realized by the things I was able to buy, people I would be surrounded by, events I would be invited to, and comfort and security I could afford myself.

I was constantly on my phone or computer responding to emails. My weeks became a predictable blur of running from the gym to work to client events to sleep. I would rinse and repeat my externally stimulated routine over and over again. I wasn't unhappy, but something seemed to be missing. Something I couldn't quite put my finger on. I was making good money, had a great job and reputation at work, had great relationships with my family and friends, got to travel to cool places and have dinner at swanky spots, my health was good, and I liked my apartment. So, what gives? I had this problem of feeling apathetic and going through the monotonous motions of another day, but how could I fix that?

While this hyper-productive view of life served me very well in some ways, looking back on this with all I know now, the symptoms of energetic imbalance couldn't be clearer. The pendulum swung too far to one end of the continuum—a focus on the physical and mental energy of the world. I was putting my power in the hands of things outside of my control. I was focused on distracting myself with incessant work, fitness, and busyness with the singular view that the more I do, the more I become. I didn't realize I was energetically and vibrationally imbalanced at the time because I didn't even know how to spot it. As a result, I was ungrounded, unaware, and unintentional with the things I did for the longest time.

At the beginning of the coronavirus pandemic in 2020, I moved to our Structured Finance Private Placements desk, still within the investment banking division. There was an opening on the team, and I was asked to step into a much bigger role. Together as just a two-person team, my boss and I would originate, structure, negotiate, sell, and allocate private debt transactions. This work was purely private-side (i.e., no public salesforce like in Lev Fin), so it was left to us to handle a significant amount of the workload as we were the only product experts in the firm.

The work was varied and exciting. I got to work on deals for building new sports stadiums around the world, structure securitizations, and raise capital for some of the largest financial institutions globally. By all means, I was learning a ton and getting incredible exposure. In just two years (and while working remotely during the pandemic), my boss and I grew the revenue of the Goldman Sachs Private Placement business a staggering 500% and I was promoted to vice president.

While I was on my very well-defined path to climb the corporate ladder in the finance world, something happened in the summer of 2020 that turned my energy upside down, inside out, and pulled my life apart in every possible way.

In June of that year, just two days after my birthday, my mom went for a routine thirty-minute outpatient thumb surgery to fix a partially torn ligament that had been bothering her for a little while. They sedated her for the procedure and couldn't arouse her after the surgery. She was intubated and rushed to the hospital where it became apparent that she was suffering from severe seizure activity in the brain. My mom spent roughly three weeks in a coma on life support in the neuro-ICU before she ultimately passed on from complications.

The shock was intense. My mom was the breadwinner, my greatest teacher, hero, role model, and the undeniable light and glue of our entire family. As my dad traveled most weeks for work and I was five years younger than my sister, the relationship I had with my mom was the source of a lot of my familial love.

The unexpected and sudden nature of her departure left our family reeling. I was filled with deep questions about myself, my life purpose, and the inherent nature of my reality. My dad was in complete shock; and my sister, a physician herself, was baffled by the case. In this dark hour, I felt like I had to step in to be a substitute for one among many of the home maintenance jobs my mom did out of love for her family, in addition to her successful professional career. I had to make sense of the entire family's finances and organization.

I had to find dozens of log-in passwords—bank accounts, mortgages, utilities, telecommunications, credit cards, insurance payments, and countless others. I had to keep payments scheduled on time; transfer accounts, titles, and deeds; provide death certificates and paperwork to dozens of providers; talk to insurance companies, employers, family, and friends. Each day was a marathon of newfound investigation in how to triage the material needs of my family to keep everything running as smoothly as possible. This stuff isn't taught in school, nor are the extent of such silent services by a parent normally recognized or even fully appreciated by their children. It truly felt like being tossed into the deep end and being asked to sink or swim. All of this happened while going through my own grieving process and coming back to my sleepless investment banking role.

In the months that followed, I started to receive insights into a world that was different from the one I was used to seeing. The first six months after she passed was a whirlwind. A whirlwind of intense pain, confusion, anger, pity, and so many other feelings. I remember I would go on runs in the morning and just break down crying in the middle of them. At night, I would wake with extreme night terrors and find myself sobbing into my pillow when I awoke. My mom's sudden and unexpected passing was the catalyst for me to turn a light back onto myself. I found myself asking the questions of "What's happening?" "What is life?" "How could this happen?" "Who am I?" "What is my and humanity's purpose here?" Things began to turn existential for me.

I had no idea the answers, but over the next two years, my journey would evolve in the deepest and most unimaginable ways.

After her passing, a switch flipped. I went deeper into meditation than I ever knew possible. Worries around me dissolved and I felt immense peace wash over me every time I sat down to meditate. My meditation practice as a banker went from having "no time," to five minutes, ten minutes, twenty minutes, and ultimately forty minutes twice a day. I was waking up at 3:33 a.m. just to fit it into my daily schedule. Yes, the feelings I would carry with me throughout my day were *that* powerful.

Within the crevasses of meditation, introspection, and solitude that the COVID-19 pandemic forced me into, I cultivated a channel of communication beyond myself and beyond this world. The signs started with numbers I noticed everywhere. They evolved into words I saw while walking down the street, and ultimately into a level of ask-and-receive communication with nearly everything in my life. I was being guided along my path, and my mom was the angel watching over me, orchestrating and sending me these signs from beyond.

During the first three months of 2021, I started to receive insights, downloads, and guidance from something completely outside of myself. It was a message telling me every single day for over ninety days, "You need to help people." I was confused and had no idea what to even make of it. Although I had meditated for well over two decades, I never had a mystical experience like this. It was almost like I was being spoken to by a guardian angel—my mom.

Here I was, on the life track I had dreamed of. I was a hard-working, left-brained Goldman Sachs investment banker. However, when these existential questions and newfound experiences started to bubble up, a different part of my brain seemed to light up with curiosity. I knew I could use the traits I learned at Goldman (resiliency, hunger for learning, analytical thinking, and discipline) to find the answers I sought. I also started attempting to communicate with these angels or guides who were sending me messages.

When I wholeheartedly put my intentions behind wanting to uncover these answers, I was slowly granted an entryway into seeing the world through an incessant dance of intertwining energies. A world where I was guided along my journey with benevolence, ease, and grace—so long as I did my best and surrendered the rest.

If you told me five years ago that I would go from spending half of all hours in the week working in finance to cultivating a dialogue with the angelic realm, I would have laughed and probably thought you were crazy. Yet somehow, I was led to learn from changemakers in every field including cognitive neuroscience, quantum physics and biology, spirituality, positive psychology, breathwork, pharmacology, and energy work.

What I got from seeing the world as energy and tapping into communication with my angel guides was an entirely new perspective on my life, my purpose, and the world around me. The wounding I experienced opened my eyes but more so opened my mind to possibility. As the great poet Rumi says, "If you are irritated by every rub, how will you be polished?"[14]

Everything I did had a compounding effect on my internal feelings of peace, calmness, trust, and joy—words you'd probably seldom expect an investment banker to embody. The thoughts I had, the words I spoke, the smallest daily habits and practices I put in place, my body posture, the food I ate, how I spent my free time, even how I chose to reframe difficult situations—made my energy feel lighter and brighter each and every day. I was choosing to take action, and I could feel the internal energy of my mind changing. Countless friends and colleagues would even mention things to me like, "Your energy is off the charts."

Through my story, my hope is that you are able to spot signs of when your energy might be out of balance without having to go through extreme life experiences like the loss of a loved one. Some of these signs that I was out of balance were:

- A monotonous routine on autopilot, done out of habit with little conscious awareness
- A lack of intention in the daily tasks I did
- Overtraining in the gym
- Filling my hours with incessant work or to-dos, with the view that only by being more productive would I yield more results
- Worrying about what others would think of me (external validation)
- Constantly finding myself saying how "busy" I was or how much I had to do
- Chasing after the external worldly goodies to make me happy (money, things, people, events, job titles)—and giving my power away to those things
- Working to just buy things and continue to feed my lifestyle—capitalism for the sake of capitalism
- Being exhausted, overwhelmed, and consistently focused on work even though I liked it

- Not making my joy my number-one priority
- Vigorously working to get to the next rank, achievement, or bonus in life to bring me happiness

My process started with *deep* self-awareness. This is the foundation of absolutely everything, and I had never been told of its importance throughout my life.

Self-awareness is fundamental for providing the base to bring forth the transcendent energetic balance you so deeply desire. Within knowing the self, you are able to know which energies are yours, and which are outside of you. This also provided a basis for me to discern when I was being sent explicit signs from my angels and the Universe.

Self-awareness involves getting vulnerable and real with yourself. From there, I removed the noise and distractions surrounding me. It allowed me to go deep into meditation, slow down, and be extremely present. I continued to invest in my personal growth after getting a taste of the results and formulated a five-pillar psychological and metaphysical journaling practice I start every day with (see Part 2). I stayed with it consistently, held myself accountable, continued to learn new tools along the way, and found a vibrant alignment within myself that has to be experienced to be truly understood. This is what I want to lead you toward.

It took the greatest tragedy in my life for me to even realize I needed to find energetic balance. But even more importantly, it took this loss for me to ultimately release, let go, and surrender into the benevolence of the Universe and my angels. Tapping into this guidance, you might feel resistance and skepticism. I did too. However, when I released my judgments of calling upon angelic guidance, it directed my path in one of the most humbling ways. Guidance from your spirit guides is one of the greatest unsung resources you can tap into—and everyone can do it.

Shortly after my mom's passing, I was given the book recommendation of Lorna Byrne's *Angels in my Hair*. The word *angel* didn't particularly resonate with me before, but her book felt like divine intervention and her story was faith inspiring. The book is Lorna's personal story of being able to communicate with and see her angel guides throughout her life in Ireland. She was illiterate, struggled financially, experienced deep personal loss and sacrifice, and ultimately allowed the light from her angels to guide her life path. It was a nice book with an interesting perspective, but I didn't immediately buy into the concept of angels after reading it. As everything becomes clearer as time passes, I can see now that the book was my introduction into the world of angels I would soon come to know very intimately.

The word *angel* can often feel tied to religious connotations. However, this isn't my intention. For me, *angel* simply means a spirit guide. Everyone who comes to Earth has one of these guides who they can call on for help. They're typically of an unseen density of light energy and will never impose on your free will. These angels or spirit guides have unconditional love for you which pours from them, and they will only act for your benevolence and the highest good of all when called upon.

I use the term *angel* because it's from my mom's passing that I awakened to the realization that I have the ability to call in this higher dimensional support and assist others in receiving their messages. My mom is one of my guardian angels, and she opened the gateway for me to uncover insights into this etheric energy world.

My intention with the chapters that follow is to show you how to realize tangible energetic benefits for yourself. Hopefully along the way, my story of communication with my angels and energetic beings of love and light will inspire you to explore your own connection to those who have passed on and the spirit guides you've been sent here with.

Everyone's path is different, and there is no one right way to live life. This is not a call to leave your job or follow my path. Rather, this is a roadmap to achieve greater fulfillment and trust in whatever path you feel called to live your life on.

More than anything, I hope you realize the energy within you. The energy you're capable of, and the inner states of peace and joy you deserve to feel. In the next section, I'll explain the first steps you can take to balance your energy and what that process looks like.

As we embark on this next phase of the journey, I offer you a grounding cord. I learned this technique from energy healer and teacher, Jeffrey Allen.[15] I created my own guided version you can follow along with from the resources at https://www.nealbakshi. com/bankingonangels.

Sit comfortably, close your eyes, and take a deep belly breath in. Imagine a tree trunk, waterfall, or beam of light descending from the base of your spine (the root chakra) deep into the center of the Earth. Breathe into it. Ask the earth energy to take away those feelings and thoughts no longer serving you, and any energies that are not yours. Watch them dissipate down your grounding cord.

Then, feel the energy of the earth replenishing you with strength and bringing you into your body and present moment.

You are here now, and you are about to unlock the formula to bring you into your greatest energetic balance yet. This balance will open your consciousness to new insights about yourself and new perspectives about the world and how to achieve all you want in it. The first step begins with knowing who you really are.

Part 1:
Practices to Balance Your Energy

Energetic balance doesn't happen tomorrow, it begins today. In this section, I'll share five introductory practices and frameworks you can use to begin to unpack and balance your energy. From generating self-awareness to removing distractions, you will start on your journey toward understanding yourself. Meditation has been a cornerstone of my life, and I'll explain to you why it's so beneficial on a number of levels and how you can begin to practice it yourself. From there, you'll get a glimpse into the importance of having a personal growth practice, and then learn how you can experiment in your own life to see what yields you the greatest results.

Come back to your intention from when you started this book. What was it? Say it out loud to yourself, and now supplement it with what you hope to take away from the next five practices.

Practice 1: Who Am I?

"Knowing your own darkness is the best method for dealing with the darknesses of other people. One does not become enlightened by imagining figures of light, but by making the darkness conscious. The most terrifying thing is to accept oneself completely. Your visions will become clear only when you can look into your own heart. Who looks outside, dreams; who looks inside, awakes."

—Carl Jung, founder of analytical psychology

A few months after my mom passed on in 2020, one of my good friends, Quiggy, came to visit me in New York. We went out and talked about my situation. He suggested I reach out to a life coach he worked with as a way to help me process my grief. I knew nothing about life coaching at the time and listened to his suggestion out of kindness but dismissed the notion of needing a coach for myself.

For the vast majority of my conscious life, I identified myself with my past. I saw the difficulties I experienced and was forced to overcome as an emotional résumé of sorts.

I struggled with foundational math and writing skills from a young age, failing kindergarten and receiving Ds in fourth grade. My temperament as a child was one filled with tantrums, angst, frustration, and stubbornness. I was obese throughout my adolescence, destroying my self-confidence for years. I had a number of serious injuries and emergency health problems, and the list goes on.

As I went through middle school, high school, college, and into the working world, I treated each of the various setbacks I experienced as mountains I had climbed to show how strong I was. I began to build my self-worth and self-esteem by internalizing the past traumas, hurts, and setbacks—looking down on them with a condescending sense of superiority.

Each new obstacle that was conquered was a feather in my cap to show myself where I came from. This compounded to build the image of who I ultimately thought I was. Little did I know the internal pain, conflict, and resentment I would brew deep inside. This ultimately restrained me from my full potential and genuine understanding of peace and calmness for decades.

So when my friend suggested I work with a life coach, I had my apprehensions. I rebutted that I was mentally strong enough, it was too expensive, and that I was capable of overcoming, healing, and growing on my own.

Quiggy didn't give up on me and persisted. He brought me back to a conversation I had with him a few days prior. We were supposed to go to deep Brooklyn to meet up with a few friends, but the Ubers were exorbitantly expensive and he was on the fence about it. I told him that although the cars were surge pricing more than usual, the cost would be worth it. I explained that the life experience and enjoyment we were going to have dancing with friends we hadn't seen in over a year would outweigh the slightly higher cost and that the money would ultimately come back over time.

He pulled a reverse Uno card on me as it related to my own healing journey and working with a coach, so it was hard to avoid the similarity in reasoning.

I marinated on the idea for weeks after he left. I read about coaching, the testimonials, and what it could offer. I slept on the idea, thinking about what exactly it was that I would want to work on or achieve during my time with a life coach.

As I mentioned earlier, all my life, my mom showered me with love. Through the difficult times I had growing up as a kid—with academics, my temperament, extracurriculars, weight, and health—she never gave up on me. She gave me so much compassion. She sacrificed her time and energy; she worked a full-time job and still dedicated hours on end to me daily. I spoke to her every day without fail. She would teach me, encourage me, and love me unconditionally through my good days and "Oscar the Grouch" days. She would always pick me up from the train station or airport and stay up late at night with me if I had to finish things—just as a beacon of strength and support. My mom's love was so strong and unwavering that it never truly occurred to me how blessed I really was. In high school, my friends would even say, "Neal, your mom is a saint."

It also never truly occurred to me where my blind spots were and where I could improve. Her love poured into me to the point of overflow. I was forever supported from outside of my own being. Yet with that, I was unaware of just how much shame and lack of self-love was within me until she was no longer around in her physical form.

Those wounds, harsh words of teasing, rejection, and bullying that I conquered my entire life were swept into the back of my shadow closet. They were never given the chance to be fully felt and integrated because I was never really taught the importance of doing so, let alone how to even go about it.

My emotional energy had been suppressed for years, if not decades. From working with and speaking to countless individuals, no one is immune from early life traumas in some way, shape, or form. These things you experience when you are unable to truly process them results in your brain creating belief systems in order to protect you from future hurt.

In the fall of 2020, I sat down to reflect on what I wanted out of life coaching. My self-confidence around body image was getting better but still wasn't great. What I didn't want to happen was my self-worth and acceptance of myself to come from my job, status, and money, as opposed to truly loving myself for who I am.

At that point, I knew what I needed to work on with a life coach: fostering deep self-love.

Almost two months after the initial discussion with my friend in New York, I decided to book a discovery call with the coach he recommended, Dara. We spoke and the vibes just felt right. I felt energized and excited from our conversation and the change I was determined to enact in my life.

Self-Awareness

No one teaches you how to truly understand yourself growing up. In school we're taught the Pythagorean theorem, how to write in cursive, the history of America in the 1800s, and how to make a volcano out of vinegar and baking soda. I'm not saying any of these things aren't worthwhile. Yet now that I'm a spiritual life coach with a stronger internal compass than I've ever felt before, it is very clear to me that an understanding of *yourself* is never made available to you in school growing up.

Through my own personal experience and in my coaching programs, deep self-awareness is the cornerstone from which all other growth and energetic alignment in your life is made possible. It's about asking the questions of "Who am I?" "What are my values?" "What are my strengths?" "What drives me?" "What do I believe?" and "Why do I believe that?" It's about spending time with yourself in a mode of reflection that you have likely seldom done before. A reflection that involves assessing your personality, learning about what makes you thrive or shy away, and hearing new perspectives from thought-provoking speakers to activate dormant neural pathways. This kind of contemplation provides you the ability to be vulnerable, open, and honest to process everything that has been stuffed away in your shadow closet for years.

Carl Jung is the founder of the school of analytical psychology and is also responsible for developing the concepts of introverted and extroverted personalities. Jung believes that the road to healing and recovery does not need to be reliving those traumatic memories or conflicts but rather a "wholehearted dedication to life."[16] What this means is that the first step on any healing or growth journey is to get a clear picture of who you are and where you are heading.

Jung states in his 1964 book, *Civilization in Transition*, "A neurosis . . . is not a disgrace . . . It is not a fatal disease, but it does grow worse to the degree that one is determined to ignore it."[17]

In life, you often fear what's behind the curtain when you take an honest look at your flaws, emotions, thoughts, or states of being. But the truth of the matter is, self-acceptance is what liberates you from the need to suppress your genuine energy from yourself or others.

Everyone has a personality, and that word derives from the Latin root *persona*, which means "mask" or "character." When you turn the light inside—behind the actor's mask—you begin to see who you are for what you are. You begin to trace back the roots of patterning and belief systems in your life. You begin to attune yourself to your internal compass, and you begin to tap into your energy in ways you never have before.

My own dedication to self-awareness, the first step of my coaching journey, showed me just how powerful this deceivingly easy task can be. My coach explained to me through Jungian psychology that when something difficult comes up for you emotionally or mentally, it is often because you're at a stage in your personal growth where you are now strong enough to handle that situation or the deeper-seated patterning behind it.

Celebrity mind architect, Peter Crone, often says, "Life will present you with people and circumstances to reveal where you are not free."[18] Viewing this with a Jungian lens, when you are presented with trying situations, it is a sign that your psyche is ready to integrate and grow past previous fears. It's ultimately up to you to decide whether you step into that fear and resistance as a pathway for growth. However, you first need to be self-aware enough to notice when this is happening and the symbolism behind it.

I challenge you to dig deep into your own self-awareness and ask yourself the deep and meaningful questions. Start with asking yourself who you are. Delve into your beliefs, your values, what you hold dear, when you feel your best, and what triggers you into patterns of fear, lack of self-worth, security, or love. What are your strengths? What do you want to lift up to become a strength? What drives you and makes you want to get up every day? These are just a few questions, but take five to ten minutes today to sit down with a pen and paper and write it out.

Separation from thought in the form of written or spoken word is crucial. The separation you create from your thoughts by putting them on paper will prevent your brain from running around in circles and giving you the illusion that it is working through processing these questions consciously.

How self-aware are you really? Come back to your energetic intention of why balance in your life is important to you and what you hope to achieve through that balance. This will help you openly and honestly dive deep into your self-awareness journey.

Practice 2: Removing Distractions

"You can always find a distraction if you're looking for one."
— Tom Kite, American professional golfer

Golf is a mental game. That's why when Tom Kite, 1992 U.S. Open Champion and World Golf Hall of Famer, talks about distractions, it carries meaning. If you're distracted, absorbed by external stimuli of what the other players are doing, how the crowd is responding, or worrying about your tee shot from four holes ago, you're going to be stuck in your head. Kite spent 175 weeks in the top ten of the Official World Golf Ranking between 1989 and 1994. That doesn't happen when you're easily distracted or unfocused.

In today's world where you are incessantly bombarded with emails, phone notifications, texts, work demands, health demands, and endless to-do lists, how can you remove the unnecessary distractions in life?

During my time in banking for eight years, I thought I was focused. Focused on my job, my health, my success, and my social circle. I would give it my all every day and feel like I was doing what I needed to get ahead in life. But the truth is, I was undeniably distracted. Distracted from creating the time, space, or energy to understand myself. Distracted from doing things with conscious intention.

My usual week as an investment banker looked like this: On Monday, I would apathetically drag myself out of bed, still nursing the hangover and exhaustion from another weekend bender of excessively late nights out. I would go through my routines of hitting the gym, going to work, and drinking loads of caffeine, all with the hope of overcoming yet another "case of the Mondays."

By Wednesday, I'd finally start feeling better. I was gradually catching up on the weekend's sleep debt (if possible) and the daily lunchtime salads were detoxing my body. But by Thursday, a client dinner or drinks event always seemed to pop up; and by Friday, I was back into full weekend-bender mode. Going out to dinner, bars, or clubs on Friday led into a hungover gym session and likely brunch on Saturday. During football season, it would even repeat on Sundays, and then we were back at Monday morning again in the blink of an eye.

It got to the point where I would have FOMO (fear of missing out) if I didn't go out with my friends. Sometimes, even if I was beyond exhausted from a week of work, I would still go out—just to stay true to plans I had made. After all, I didn't want to miss out on a night to blow off steam and experience potential stories we'd talk about for weeks to come.

My physical body was giving me immediate feedback about my energy, but I refused to listen to it. I didn't become aware of this patterning until I started working with my life coach. Only then I was able to see that I was actually avoiding things within myself, rather than taking the time to pause, understand, and integrate.

It's important to go out and have fun, no doubt. It provides a level of somatic release and enjoyment with which life deserves to be lived. However, in the New York City finance world, the nights out are regular and incessant. This unhealthy patterning wasn't even apparent to me because of how widespread it was among my friends and colleagues.

An incredible life coaching tool I learned from world-renowned coach Jay Shetty during my certification at his school was the Wheel of Life. The Wheel of Life was invented in the 1960s by Paul J. Meyer, the founder of the Success Motivation Institute and a pioneer in the self-improvement industry. It's designed to deepen self-awareness and help audit an individual's life.

A study of over 4,000 life coaching interventions at the IRS University of Southern Denmark concluded that those instances where the Wheel of Life were used reported improved self-insight, self-esteem, energy, and motivation.

Life is an interconnected wheel with all areas of your life having some impact on the other areas. The way the exercise works is a circle split into the various core areas of your life — career, finances, family, health, and so on. After doing subjective personal reflective work on where you are in each area, you quantify where you currently are and where you want to get to. You can then dig in and see if what you're doing is aligned with getting you there and where you are veering off course. As a result, you start to see positive ripple effects across the other areas of your life as various distractions are removed.

Going out and drinking, partying, and distracting myself every night of the weekend was me looking for the next shiny object to satisfy my desire to be preoccupied, busy, and doing things. It took an audit of my life for me to disentangle the root from the symptoms.

A problem in one area of life can stunt growth in another area too. When one area is out of balance, other areas frequently are as well. The same can be said with the various energetic bodies we have. Spiritual energetic growth (searching for higher purpose, leaving a legacy, contribution, feeling optimism, faith, hope, and self-actualization) is usually accomplished once other areas in life are first addressed.

As a coach, I've noticed these instances in my clients as well. The CFO of a multimillion-dollar healthcare technology startup came to me with the hopes of addressing his personal relationship concerns. After diving into an in-depth audit of his life, it became apparent that the strain on his relationship was a result of energetic imbalance in other areas of his life. Primarily, in recent years, his priority of physical health declined and his own personal growth journey had stalled. Once these areas started to improve, and he dug deeper into his own energetic balance and lifelong limiting beliefs, he naturally began to see improvements in his relationship and, consequently, with his own connection to his spiritual being.

Ultimately, auditing your life is just one of the first steps toward removing distractions. Overthinking and external stimuli keep you preoccupied from the difficult work of getting to know yourself deeply. Whether it's being trapped in patterns of overthinking about situations, worrying about what someone will think of you, or being on-the-go nonstop to feel like you're being productive, the noise and distractions can take any number of forms.

After auditing my own life and going through my self-love healing journey, spirituality became my number-one focus. I wanted to deepen my understanding of the metaphysical world to understand what really happened to my mom's soul and how I could still receive messages from her. I sought out answers, explanations, facts, and reasonings—both physically, but also on a deeper level. A level I was already sensing things in, and that was the spiritual energetic level.

Removing Distractions to Notice the Signs

From my own personal experience, once I was able to address the incessant flow of distractions in my life, I was able to be more present to notice the signs the Universe was sending me along my daily routines.

One of the most striking things that started to happen to me was the sudden astute observation of repeating angel numbers. For some, it feels more comfortable to refer to repeating numbers as just that. However, my story evolved differently. I only started noticing the number patterns after my mom passed on, and it wasn't just a once-in-a-while occurrence. I used my logical mind along with my intuition to piece together the puzzle from there. Over time, I started to receive guidance, insights, and answers to my questions through noticing the numbers. My guardian angels were trying to send me messages in plain sight—through these angel numbers. The feelings and phenomena increased with frequency and intensity the more I noticed them and celebrated noticing them.

I'm a logical-thinking, left-brained person who has worked with numbers my entire life. From majoring in economics in college to working in finance for my career, I take my numbers seriously.

I started noticing the numbers on license plates, building addresses, flight numbers, departure times, sidewalk graffiti, distance or arrival time to a destination on the GPS, weather temperature numbers, totals on my dinner receipts, on the sides of trucks driving by in New York City, my Venmo balance, phone numbers, the number of Instagram comments or likes on a post, gas station signs, my Apple Health step counter, the treadmill during workouts, and on financial price moves on CNBC and my Bloomberg terminal.

After months of brushing them off as coincidence in late 2020, I could no longer avoid the symbolism staring me in the face at every corner of my daily life.

I voraciously sifted through Google articles and numerology sites to discern a meaning or a framework to follow. As the weeks and months wore on in 2021, I began to get a better grasp of what I was experiencing and why.

If you're interested in the way I decoded angel numbers, you can download my Angel Number Decoder from https://www.nealbakshi.com/bankingonangels. Different numbers can mean different things to different people. Just like any language, it's important to also cultivate your own style, usage, and understanding of it.

By the spring of that year, I started looking at shop windows and seeing specific written signs of things I was thinking about in that moment being reflected back at me—a Mother's Day sale message, reminders about taking care of myself, motivational phrases, and things I had been putting off that needed to be addressed.

As things progressed still, I decided to experiment and ask for specific signs. One spring day, I was going from NYC to Hoboken.

Feeling particularly curious about whether my guides were listening to me, I asked to see a tall man with dark hair wearing a blue baseball cap on the PATH train platform. I thought this was an obscure enough request as I left my apartment midday. Sure enough, twenty minutes later, out of only ten people taking the train at that time, there was a man over six feet with jet black hair wearing a blue baseball cap standing on the platform next to me.

Here's another example. One morning I woke up feeling in a funk. I went for a run and asked, "How can I be more confident?" As I got a mile and a half in, I saw a motivational message written out in chalk on the running path from the day before. It read, "You got this, keep going!"

Each time I would text my sister and brother-in-law in disbelief with the signs the Universe and my angels were giving me. It was fantastical to imagine such strong synchronicities were being divinely guided to me. With hundreds of experiences such as these over the past two years, my well of spiritual faith deepened substantially. I began to trust in the intelligence of all that is around me as the right clients were guided into my life, my coaching practice grew, and my path was telling me to be in service to others.

Some of the common ways distractions show up in your life are through your thoughts (fears, doubts, judgments) and the need for external validation (doing what others do to be liked and accepted). In their more tangible forms, they can include mindless and excessive scrolling on social media, endless swiping on dating apps, junk food, overtraining at the gym, an unending and busy work schedule, or inordinately turning to weed, alcohol, partying, or pornography.

When you clear away the distractions and noise, you create an avenue for your inner voice to come through. You allow it to develop, strengthen, and feel heard. This is when the magic starts to happen and you begin to *feel* your intuition strengthen. This is you tapping into your deeper and more subtle energy.

Jeffrey Allen, the international energy healer and teacher, walks through four steps to reading energy in his Duality training. These steps can also be adapted to turning down the noise and distractions in your life. The first step is to close your eyes and focus your attention. Next, you imagine that there is a knob, which is your analyzer of the outside world. Get a sense of where that is for you right now on a scale of 0–100, 100 being heavily analyzing the outside world with thoughts. Then, slowly and consciously turn that dial down, all the way to 0. This is you energetically turning down the constant need to analyze the noise and distractions of the physical world. You don't always get completely rid of the distractions, but the goal is that they fade away and are far off in the background. Third, you open your mind to curiosity and remain patient. Without effort, and while continuing to release the distractions, you last receive the insights.[19]

Turning down and removing distractions is how angel numbers and signs began popping out to me everywhere. Essentially, turning down the external noise is what you do in meditation—and meditation will change your life.

Practice 3: Meditation Will Change Your Life

"Don't feel badly if you find yourself too restless to meditate deeply. Calmness will come in time, if you practice regularly. Just never accept the thought that meditation is not for you. Remember, calmness is your eternal, true nature."
— Paramahansa Yogananda, yogi and guru, founder of Self-Realization Fellowship

I grew up in a very spiritual family and started meditating at the age of five. I didn't realize it at the time, but I was beyond blessed to be raised on Paramahansa Yogananda's path of Self-Realization Fellowship (SRF). The core precepts of his teachings are self-realization through scientific methods of meditation and spiritualizing your daily life.

Paramahansa Yogananda was an Indian yogi and guru who introduced millions of people to the teachings of meditation and the ancient yogic science of Kriya Yoga. He was one of the most influential forces for bringing meditation and spirituality to America in the 1920s, and his book *Autobiography of a Yogi* sold well over four million copies.

In fact, Steve Jobs, cofounder and CEO of Apple, first read Yogananda's *Autobiography of a Yogi* as a teenager. He then reread it when he went to India in 1974, and every year up until his passing. It was the only book Jobs kept on his iPad, and all attendees present at his funeral received a copy of the book as they walked out.[20]

Unlike Steve Jobs, however, I wasn't all-in on spirituality as a teenager—even having grown up on the spiritual path. I treated going to meditate with my parents like I did karate. It was something I did out of obligation for my parents as opposed to my own intrinsic motivation.

Growing up, my mom would always say I was a very excitable kid. I was easily triggered by situations, causing me to feel intense emotions, and I would react hyperbolically and immediately. Tantrums, fits, anger, stubbornness, facetiousness, and any other less-than-appreciated response you can imagine, I displayed it.

I continued to meditate from childhood throughout my entire life. It taught me how to sit still and not respond to every itch. It showed me how to begin to quiet my mind and focus my attention, will, and concentration. Ultimately, these intense emotional reactions dissipated over the years of practice. Between the ages of five and twenty-eight, I didn't really experience any altered states of consciousness in meditation. However, when my mom was admitted into the neuro-ICU in 2020, that started to change.

I remember every day for those nearly three weeks that my mom was in the hospital, my dad, sister, brother-in-law, dog, and I would sit down and mediate together. We'd meditate for hours throughout the day and send her healing energy.

Dinners and other moments throughout the day were shrouded with worried silence; no one knew what to say. However, it was the meditations throughout the day that always seemed to bring us back to a better place of peace and faith.

Prior to those family meditations, I had never been firmly intentional with my practice. This was quite literally a life-and-death situation, and I was going to do my best to make this a life situation. I started to see symbols, feel her presence, and experience expansive light through these healing meditations.

We did our best, but ultimately, her traumatic brain injuries and ceaseless seizure activity was an affliction even my angelic mother could not overcome. After these experiences, however, I realized just how powerful meditation can be and what I was capable of unlocking as part of it.

For the first six months after her passing, through the end of 2020, my intentions with my meditations were around helping to provide me answers, solace, peace, strength, and resolution. I meditated every morning for ten to fifteen minutes, eventually working my way up to twenty minutes.

While I was seeing some benefits, it wasn't until the turn of the calendar year that things really kicked into high gear for me. For the first three months of 2021, work was incessant. I mean truly incessant. Clocking the hours didn't even do justice anymore. In the height of the COVID pandemic, we were working from home and busier than ever. I worked every day, including weekends, for those three months. We were a two-person team on the Private Placement desk—selling the largest billion-dollar deals our market had ever seen and doing six deals at a time.

Throughout it all, I kept up my meditation practice. Every morning, instead of asking for solace, I asked for guidance. I asked for what steps I needed to take and what I needed to do. "Please guide me" became the mantra I would use in meditation.

Every morning as I would do this, I would get a response. It was a deep inner calling, a felt-sense of incredible emotion from my heart, saying to me, "You need to help people."

For three straight months, I received this same message. "You need to help people, you need to help people, you need to help people."

I had no idea what that even meant or how I was supposed to go about doing that. My entire life I thought I was supposed to be an investment banker. I *wanted* to be an investment banker. Now I was supposed to help people? Was that through my banking role somehow?

As I was receiving these insights in early 2021, a good friend from my college days at NYU, Leah, who had also suddenly lost a parent years prior, reached out to me in support. As we got to talking, she asked me what my gifts were that I could share with others, or what people came to me with throughout my life. I started to recall patterns of people coming to me for help, guidance, and advice. I asked around, and my friends said they appreciated my wisdom, empathetic, and non-judgmental nature.

I had no idea what to even do with this information, so I went back to my life as a banker and let the days pass by. As they did, my daily meditation practice expanded from twenty minutes in the morning to twenty minutes in the morning and evening. Ads for life coaching certifications and personal development courses started popping up in my social media newsfeeds. I ignored them as I do most ads, but something eventually piqued my interest: The Jay Shetty Certification School.

I had followed Jay for some time, read his book, and really resonated with his work. I took his intro course and absolutely loved it. From there, I tore through his minimum 120-hour curriculum and went above and beyond the number of live coaching and supplementary coursework hours needed to graduate. I wrapped up the certification in less than a few months over the summer of that year. Coaching felt natural—like I was in a state of flow, and I genuinely enjoyed it. While this was happening, Leah coached me into creating my business from scratch. All of this transpired while I was still working a full-time investment banking job, and we were having a record year. I was working more than I ever had before yet was more energized and focused than I had been in years.

It felt like meditation was supercharging my ability to get everything accomplished. By the end of the summer, I was meditating forty minutes each morning and evening. I was so hooked on the results I was getting from meditation that I would wake up at 3:33 a.m. (angel number) just to be able to fit my practice into my busy work schedule. It became as integral as working out, showering, and eating breakfast. It made me feel peaceful, calm, clear-headed, more "in flow," and less emotionally reactive.

I started meditating right before my coaching sessions. I found that it helped me tap into my intuition to ask my clients the right guiding questions. Everything seemed to be falling into place.

As I look back, I see this all started as a result of meditation. I was guided back to my college friend to help me make sense of my gifts and push me out of my comfort zone. The right certifications came into my path. Clients started to flow to me immediately, and they saw real results. I share this story to show that my entire life changed because of those deeply internalized states of meditation. I received guidance from beyond myself, took note of the signs, and did the best with the opportunities presented to me from there.

The Latin root of *meditation* derives from the word *meditari*, which means to consider, contemplate, or reflect on. With so many forms of meditation today, it's easy to get confused about where to start. It can also be easy to get disgruntled and disheartened when you don't see the immediate results you desire or that others speak about. However, what it first and foremost comes down to is removing the distractions we talked about previously. Once those distractions are out of the way, all it takes is sitting with yourself, basically doing nothing for two to five minutes to start. You don't need to try to control your thoughts or stop thinking, but rather just sit there with yourself. Once you feel you have sufficiently perfected the "do nothing" phase and are ready for the next level of meditation, head over to https://www.nealbakshi.com/bankingonangels and download my free Beginner's Guide to Meditation. This is the next step within your meditation journey to concentrate your willpower.

A Buddhist monk once explained meditation using the analogy of sitting by a highway with cars passing by from either direction. In meditation, you are the observer on the side of the highway, and the cars passing by are your thoughts. Any time you find yourself getting fixated on one of the cars passing by, gently, with compassion, say to yourself, "Thank you, thinking" and pull yourself back to simply observing the highway in its entirety. By thanking and acknowledging the thought, you are recognizing it instead of suppressing it. This helps it to continue on instead of stopping and causing a traffic jam.

Thinking is the main purpose of the brain, just as breathing is the main purpose of the lungs. In the early stages of your meditation journey, it can simply be about observing the thoughts. By observing the thoughts, you create what Michael A. Singer talks about in his *New York Times* #1 best-selling book, *The Untethered Soul*, as the subject-object relationship. You are the subject (or observer) that is aware of the thoughts you have. You are not the thoughts, but rather, you are simply aware of them.[21] Once you are able to first observe them from that seat of your higher self, you can then detach your intimate association with them. You as the observer have awareness, consciousness, and a sense of existence. You exist regardless of if your thoughts are there or not.

The more you pull back into this consciousness, the more your thoughts, emotions, and world become something you're watching. As Singer goes on to portray, "[The world] keeps changing, but there's no sense of it being a problem. The more you are willing to just let the world be something you're aware of, the more it will let you be who you are—the awareness, the Self, the Atman, the Soul."[22]

Brainwaves

For science-minded people like myself, research on brainwaves and neurochemicals shows the actual technical explanation behind meditation and mindfulness. It proves why dropping into deeper meditative states helps to reduce stress and slow down your brain's frequency—literally.

Brainwaves are synchronized electrical signals in your neurons. They have a rhythm and speed at which they fire, and the frequency is the time that elapses between one cycle and the next. This frequency is measured in hertz (Hz). When my mom was in a coma, the neurologists were monitoring her brainwave activity on an electroencephalogram (EEG). The EEG has small sensors attached to the scalp and picks up the electrical signals produced by the brain.[23] In my mom's case, the goal was to completely suppress her brain's seizure activity in the hopes of "restarting" her brain with normal function. Through observing the EEG by her hospital bed and the bursts of electrical signals it recorded, it became very clear to me that our very own thoughts are measurable energetic impulses in the tangible form of electricity.

Science has shown us that the five key brainwave states of the human brain are beta, alpha, theta, delta, and gamma.[24]

Learning about the relationship between brainwaves and meditation, you bring awareness to knowing where your mental frequency is when you feel stressed or overwhelmed. Once you can consciously identify it, you can treat it with gratitude for how it served you, release it, and make the choice to pull yourself into a calmer state of mind through practices like meditation and breathwork.

1. Beta (~12–38 Hz) is the conscious and waking mind. It is the objective, action-driven state you are in when you go about your day—problem-solving, decision-making, and focused on activity. On the higher end of the spectrum, it is the elevated state you find yourself in when you are in high anxiety, stressful situations, or overthinking. Operating too much in high beta takes a tremendous amount of energy and causes tension throughout the body.

2. Alpha, one level deeper (~8–12 Hz), is when the brain is idling. It's when you're taking a break, resting, and deeply relaxed. It's the feeling of drifting where you're not tethered to reality just before falling asleep. This state is also called your "center" to some, meaning there's no concept of time-space and you are aligned to your inner consciousness. Techniques around creative visualization, body healing, and peace thrive at this level of the mind. This level can easily be triggered through guided techniques, is a more "active" form of meditation, and can be accessed as you go about your daily tasks.

3. Theta (~3–8 Hz) is your subconscious mind. This is the state you are experiencing in deep meditation or rapid eye movement (REM) sleep with vivid dreams. It is in this brainwave state that those with strong intuitive or psychic abilities have been observed tapping into their gifts. Interestingly, the primary resonant electromagnetic frequency of planet Earth, known as the Schumann resonance (7.83 Hz), falls into this band.

4. Delta (~0.5–3 Hz) is the level of even deeper meditation or non-rapid eye movement (NREM) sleep, where breathing slows along with muscle activity and heartbeat. Delta has also been linked to connections with higher intelligence by some researchers.

5. Last, and least understood by today's research, is the gamma state (~38+ Hz). This state has been observed through EEGs of monks who have meditated for over ten thousand hours. It is a state of creativity, bliss, inspiration, and happiness. It incorporates aspects from all different areas of the brain and

is just starting to be unveiled. It is speculated that gamma modulates perception and consciousness, which leads to spiritual emergence.

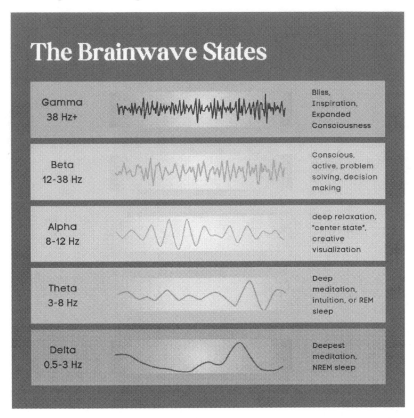

Dawson Church, PhD, has been hailed as a breakthrough researcher in the field of epigenetics. His book, *The Genie in Your Genes*, along with other research, touches on the various brainwave states and neurochemicals in the brain. He found that in states of "flow" or congruence in the body (heart, breath, and mind coherence), you have increased theta and delta waves—associated with deep meditation.[25]

In these states, he also found that the brain's prefrontal cortex shuts down, consistent with the brainwave states of mystics who have been meditating for thousands of hours in their lifetime. The prefrontal cortex is one of the three areas of the brain which makes up the Default Mode Network (DMN). The DMN is commonly considered to be where the "ego"—our sense of self—resides. This includes planning, decision-making, memory, attention, emotions, body image, and language. When this shuts down, it means that self-absorbed thinking ceases, beta (waking) brainwaves almost disappear, alpha (relaxation) increases, and delta and theta (deep meditation) increase dramatically.

Harvard researcher, Teresa Amabile, found that those who spent time in elevated flow states noticed the effects persist for the next forty-eight hours. People in these states were five times more productive, and according to a U.S. government study, saw an increase of 490% in their problem-solving abilities.[26]

Alpha brainwaves are the bridge that connects your beta waking brain to the deeper levels of theta and delta. This is where techniques like creative visualization thrive and you can begin to implant positive affirmations into your subconscious. The best part about the alpha brainwave state is that you can consciously pull yourself into it—even with your eyes open—to co-create your reality from a calm and centered state.

In deeper states of meditation, delta waves become the springboard into big gamma waves. During a compassion meditation, Church cites that gamma brainwave activity went up nearly 700% from the baseline observed.[27] Gamma is currently considered to be the brainwave of geniuses; and while research is still ongoing, the ability for monks and mystics to tap into this state of mind shows that there is some profound insight to be gained from deep states of meditation.

Understanding the brainwaves provides scientific proof that meditation can help your brain slow down and take you out of stressful high-beta states. Next time you find yourself getting excessively worked up, bring awareness to your breath and mind, and see if you can consciously bring yourself down to a less intense mental state.

Focusing on your breathing helps with this, and there are two techniques you can try. One is 4:8 breathing. This means breathing in for four counts and out for eight counts. The second is 4:7:8 breathing, which is in for four counts, holding for seven counts, and out for eight counts. When the heart, breath, and brain are in coherence, you are able to enter states of flow. Understanding the brainwaves helps to understand how and why you can access these higher states of consciousness to bring you deeper peace, calmness, and clarity in your everyday life.

In guided creative visualization, energy merging, and manifestation exercises, I guide my clients into an alpha state where they can work with the power of their mind to intentionally design and create the outcomes they desire. It has been such an effective practice for me, that I now block off fifteen minutes on my calendar a day to consciously drop into the alpha state and visualize the outcomes I desire.

I've come to realize that the "ego mind" often looks for reasons to understand why things actually work before believing they will work. In seeing the science behind metaphysical acts like meditation, it allows you to reduce egoic resistance and drop into these states of mind with greater belief. Belief that the practices you put into place in your life will work is over half the process.

The Universe and the brain respond most effectively to feelings, so it's about creating the vivid felt-sense of emotions in the body to allow this to truly take hold. When you feel it, you can believe it and magnetize it toward you. Taking a deeper look at the neurochemicals and hormones in the body shows you how you can consciously create that felt-sense in the body and mind to make your meditations and visualizations more powerful.

According to Dawson Church, there are seven core chemical messengers in the brain that can be activated during meditation to achieve a state of deep bliss.[28] Knowing how and when neurochemicals and hormones are released in the body can help you to choose activities and emotions to regulate your internal states and bring you into higher vibrational states consciously—both in meditation and in your daily life.

1. Dopamine: The Motivational Molecule

    In alpha state meditations of creative visualization, you bring all five senses into visualizing the outcome you strongly desire. Studies have shown that effective meditation can raise dopamine in the brain by 65%, keeping you motivated to achieve your outcomes.[29]

2. Oxytocin: The Hug Drug

   This love hormone can be consciously released in a compassion meditation and is associated with the long, slow brainwaves of delta and a tribal sense of belonging. Benefits of oxytocin are linked to feelings of unconditional love, emotional intimacy, and lowering stress and anxiety.

3. Norepinephrine: The Attention Focuser

   Your body naturally produces norepinephrine when it is in fight-or-flight mode, so it is important to find its balance. This can bring you into focused states of flow and balanced alertness to help you stay focused on the object of your meditation.

4. Serotonin: The Satisfaction Molecule

   Serotonin has a similar chemical structure to psilocybin and as such has been linked to hallucinations in deep states of meditation—which mystics such as St. Francis of Assisi or Radha Krishna have been believed to achieve. It also plays a key role in mood, sleep, digestion, and healing.

5. Nitric Oxide (NO): The Intensity Powerhouse

   Nitric Oxide is produced by nasal breathing. During meditation or breathwork, it improves brain neuroplasticity, which contributes to your ability to modify or remove limiting beliefs.

6. Beta-Endorphin: Body Ecstasy

   Beta-Endorphin is one of the most pleasurable substances

in the human brain and is behind the rush you get from working out. When Beta-Endorphin is released, physical distractions fall away and you are left with a deep sense of well-being in the body. This is why some expert meditators are able to feel no pain when put under physical stress, like walking on hot coals or sharp objects.

7. Anandamide: The Bliss Molecule

The Sanskrit word *Ananda* literally translates to "bliss." It is felt when you are able to achieve a flow state when working and get lost in what you do. Time seems to fly by and you are in a state of pure bliss, joy, relaxation, and ecstasy. This is likely why some highly advanced yogis can meditate for hours or even days.

Through research, Church found that various parts of the brain shut down in ecstatic states associated with meditation. This includes the DMN (your ego mind) as well as the region that locates your body in space. Thus, in the brains of highly trained meditators, they become no one, nowhere, and the brain simultaneously floods with oxytocin and immense love.

Looking back at my fast-paced and demanding job at Goldman Sachs, I would always have people asking me, "Neal, how are you so calm all the time?" My answer would be simple: "I meditate." My colleague would usually shake their head, roll their eyes, and go back to work. Having consistently noticed the results though, the empirical evidence of my inner peace and calmness in the face of intense life events points directly to my daily habit of meditation. Understanding the science of why that is reinforces my belief in it all the more.

Dr. Amishi Jha, a cognitive neuroscientist at the University of Miami, recently published a number of studies and conclusions she reached in her 2021 book, *Peak Mind*. In her research, U.S. military personnel were taught a mindfulness meditation technique. She found that those who meditated twelve minutes or more a day saw a noticeable and measurable improvement in their quality of life and concentration.[30]

Meditation has been around for millennia. Ancient cultures, scriptures, and traditions have exalted its transcendental capacity for just as long. It is just now that modern science is able to shine the slightest light as to what is happening in the brain and body during meditation, and this is still just the tip of the iceberg.

Nassim Haramein is the world leader in unified physics with over thirty-five years of research across the fields of physics, mathematics, cosmology, geometry, quantum mechanics, biology, chemistry, and anthropology. In one of his famous quotes, he states, "Spirituality is the physics that we haven't yet understood."[31]

Recently, my dad told me a story that when my parents came to the United States over forty years ago, yoga was a little-known form of movement in the West. Today, you can't drive past a strip mall on the highway without seeing a yoga studio. Similarly, as the doors of possibility open through meditation, the benefits and experiences you *feel* through personal practice will lead you to deep inner peace.

If you're new to meditation, try a two-to-five-minute practice and set a challenge for yourself to do it consistently for a certain number of days. If you're more experienced, see if you can add on more time, another session, greater consistency, or deeper concentration.

Practice 4: Invest in Your Personal Growth

"Life is a game of spiritual evolution, not circumstantial comfort."
—Peter Crone, celebrity coach

At what age were you taught about personal growth? Did anyone take the time to explain what it genuinely means, why it's important, and how it can help you gain better grounding?

Working at Goldman Sachs, I told myself I had no time for personal growth. My personal growth was my dedication to my job and my success in my seat. It was measured by how quickly I could climb the ranks and show the world what I was capable of. My personal growth became tied to my professional growth. Sure, I liked to take care of my physical health and read the occasional book on vacation, but personal growth extends far beyond that. Once I started to open myself to the world of coaching and personal development, I realized how expansive and beneficial it was.

After I started my coaching certification, I would receive targeted ads for a personal development platform called Mindvalley multiple times a day. I ignored them for months, thinking that the talking head on the ads, Vishen Lakhiani, could offer me no incremental value and that my life was already too busy to sign up for yet another yearly subscription.

Eventually, I received a targeted ad for one of their courses titled "Super Reading," taught by Jim Kwik, a brain coach and speedreading teacher. Growing up, I had struggled with academics in almost all areas. I had tutors for math, reading, writing, and would go to tutoring centers regularly for afterschool and summer education. I was a slow reader and even struggled to finish the reading comprehension section of the SAT in time.

Around this time, I was getting bombarded by book recommendations from friends and family as I was jumping into the coaching industry. There was so much for me to read and take in, but I was at a loss with how I could get through it all at my current reading pace. Eventually I decided to bite the bullet and begrudgingly sign up for the course. I guess this was going to propel my professional growth after all.

Mindvalley is predicated on microlearning modules, which are five-to-twenty-minute video modules daily. They build up to deliver you a course in anywhere from a week to a few months depending on the topic and teacher. In my twenty-one days taking the speedreading course, I more than doubled my reading speed. I was shocked at the progress I saw and wanted to see what else they offered.

In the months that followed, I took courses on money, meditation, energy healing, creative visualization, business growth, focus and removing distractions, tapping and emotional freedom techniques (EFT), and physical fitness.

Month after month as I continued to habit stack my microlearning time in my morning routine, I saw a new Neal come through. I learned new tools and techniques to incorporate into my daily life and my coaching practice. I found myself growing more than just professionally. I was sharing new ideas with others and reaching for new goals I never knew I wanted.

The results were addicting and fun. It was like looking in the mirror after months of diet and exercise. However, these results started to shine through in my mindset, approach, and perspective. My belief systems around what's possible for me began to expand, negative thought patterns began to dissipate, and I learned new meditation and energy techniques to share with others. Just like feeling the strength in your arms increase, I could *feel* the results of my personal growth. I felt lighter, more confident, and more capable.

As a result, my fervent passion for personal growth and development started to take form. I got in-tune with the deepest parts of what made me, me. I found greater peace through what I was learning about myself and releasing from my past.

I started to read voraciously, join masterclasses to learn more, and work with various coaches and subject matter experts across meditation, physics, biology, mindset, synchronicity, manifestation, breathwork, sound and energy healing, astrology, angelology, and business to elevate myself toward attaining my spiritual and material goals.

I perfected practices and even started to develop my own techniques of intertwining meditation, visualization, energy healing, breathwork, angel readings, and reflective journaling practices to create a bespoke coaching framework. I gave my clients the resources, tools, and space to explore what their own spiritual essence meant to them. Tapping into the deepest parts of themselves allowed them to realize soul-driven perspective shifts to tangibly achieve their goals in their careers, relationships, physical health, and emotional well-being.

I stumbled upon personal growth, but ultimately took the initiative to prioritize it. My schedule was busy with two full-time jobs (investment banking and coaching), but I made the decision to get up twenty minutes earlier to dedicate myself to my personal growth. Once I set my intentions and watered those seeds, they grew every other area of my life as a result (the Wheel of Life theory at work again). Personal growth helped me to set and tackle my goals with competency and consistency. I tapped into new energy that showed me how to see the bigger picture, be less reactive, and tap into higher levels of performance. I was less triggered by ungrateful work emails and cultivated conscious, mutually respectful, and healthy boundaries.

The list can go on, but throughout all of this, I found out why personal growth matters. I worked with others who held me accountable, and that's what I do with the clients I work with too. The high-aspiring self-starters I work with all cite accountability as a key motivating factor in their life—it keeps them moving steadily toward their goals and dream outcomes. Accountability helps you put practical action steps in place toward achieving the outcomes you desire most and will challenge your comfort zone to get you there.

Personal growth isn't just about doing things that you feel like you *have* to do. You can have a desire to grow in any area you are interested in and feel called to grow in. Personal growth means you are taking conscious action in ways that you find are beneficial to you as an individual. That can be through learning money management, energy healing, and neuroscience, or knitting and DJing. It's important to lean into joy and the things that light you up. There is no one way to do this. Mindvalley worked for me, but you can also Google a new article a day, watch a video that helps you learn nuances or new perspectives around your hobby or passion, read five pages of a book, write in a reflective journal, cook a new recipe, or reach out to someone who has knowledge that interests you; there are so many ways you can grow in ways that are fun and enjoyable to you.

How Coaches Can Help

In 1952, Florence Chadwick jumped into the Pacific Ocean from Catalina Island. She was attempting to swim to the mainland California coast, twenty-two miles away through open waters.[32] Over the previous two years, she became the first woman to swim the English Channel in both directions and set a woman's world record of thirteen hours and twenty-three minutes for one of the legs.[33]

This time in California, she was accompanied by a team beside her in boats whose job it was to look out for sharks and assist in any medical emergencies or injuries. The weather was foggy and cold, and she could hardly see the boats next to her. Fifteen hours into her swim, she started to doubt her ability to make it. Florence voiced her concerns to her mother who was in one of the boats next to her, but her mom urged her to keep going as she was likely close but could not see the finish line due to the thick fog.

About an hour later, the distance swimmer asked to be pulled out. As she rode in the boat toward shore, she soon found that she was less than half a mile from her finish line. Had she continued to keep swimming for just a little longer, she would have completed her feat.

This story reminds me of the importance of having a coach. Imagine you're driving a car. While you are self-directed toward your visions and goals in the driver's seat, a life coach provides a birds-eye, third-party, non-judgmental view of your situation. In this sense, a coach is like a drone flying overhead, telling you where the various roads and turns are, if there are any hazards in the way, helping you reroute when necessary, and pushing you through the final half mile. Had Florence Chadwick had a drone overhead coaching her along the way, she would have been guided through the fog and motivated to finish the last 3 percent of her journey.

Chadwick reattempted the swim two months later. This time, when the same dense fog set in, she kept the mental image of the shoreline in her mind and succeeded in swimming to shore.

Having a coach allows you to get organized and reach your goals more intentionally. Along the way, you gain greater awareness and open up neural pathways to new perspectives and life-changing habits. Much like personal training coaches, you learn the tools you need to feel confident in continuing your personal growth journey on your own.

A vice president I worked with in the financial services industry attested to the tools he learned as one of his greatest takeaways. After we finished working together in the coaching container, he said, "Undoubtedly, what I value most though, even more than our sessions together, was Neal's ability to provide me the tools and skills I needed to continue on in my journey."

The tools aren't just physical actions you take but growth mindsets, more balanced emotions, clearer thoughts, and rewired old beliefs. He went on to say of the experience, "Compassion for oneself; leaning into the chaos that is life; finding happiness in pursuit—and not the other way around; learning tools to find calm and peace, and find strength within myself; and simply realizing that all I needed to do was turn my sails to catch the wind; these are but a few of the takeaways from my time working with Neal."

Personal growth means continually leveling up. It means operating at a higher level across all of your energetic bodies, and in turn, raising your vibrational frequency. People often say, "The best thing you can do for me is work on yourself." Similarly, "Your vibe attracts your tribe."

When you get to the root of what those sayings actually mean, you find that within personal growth and development, you awaken dormant energy within you that allows you to elevate yourself physically, emotionally, mentally, and spiritually. Once you unlock these new energetic frequencies within yourself, you begin to attract the people, circumstances, and situations that match those frequencies. After all, most of life is simply a reflection of our internal states of being.

One technique I infuse in my coaching to help raise the level of vibrational energy for my clients is guided breathwork. Breathwork is a technique where you consciously connect with your breath in rhythmic breathing and breath retention sequences to create states of heart-mind coherence, embed empowering new beliefs, and release past traumas. After I led a session for a client, he said, "Neal's breathwork session was incredible and helped me process and rework existing thought patterns to become the best version of myself. Through guided breathwork and meditation, Neal assisted me in unlocking my fullest potential by working through limiting beliefs and ultimately manifesting the best version of myself."

Another way to grow and cultivate higher vibrational states is by paying attention to your inputs. What are you consuming? What news, media, food, friendships, environment, and conversations are entering your five sensory systems? All of these inputs have an energetic correlation to your own energetic vibration.

As Einstein once said, "We can't solve problems by using the same kind of thinking we used when we created them."[34] If you're not getting to the end result you know is meant for you, it's time to reevaluate your inputs. Nothing changes if you don't, and it starts by taking a look at the energy you're consuming in all forms.

When I started to fuel myself with personal growth energy, I started to receive just that in return. It started with the books I read, the guided meditations I listened to, the foods I ate, the changemakers I surrounded myself with, and the conscious intention I put out into the world.

If everything is energy, then the energy you consume has a direct correlation to the energy you feel, embody, and release.

Asking myself *why* has always allowed me to come back to the energy and intention behind my actions. Is your why serving you and allowing you to get where you want to go, or is it feeding back into past conditioning, self-limiting beliefs, and patterns that come from a place of lack?

Personal development and choosing higher energetic vibrations are lifelong processes—there is no limit to your growth ceiling. Take stock of what you're consuming in all areas of your life. Get to the root of why you're absorbing those inputs and if they're aligned with where you want to go. Start to tweak them as necessary and see where things change to brighten your energy and lift your internal vibratory states.

Investing money, time, and energy in certain ways helps you to achieve external benefits. On the other hand, when you take the time to invest in your personal growth and evolution, inner peace and greater fulfillment arise.

As I went deeper in personal growth, spiritual growth naturally followed suit. The signs I was noticing from my angels and spirit guides started to evolve. I would go for runs in the early morning and see five to ten feathers on the ground each day. Just when I needed an afternoon pick-me-up, I would notice rainbows refracted through glass while sitting at my desk at work (sometimes in tandem with a repeating angel number on the clock). When listening to Spotify on shuffle, a certain message was somehow always expressed to me when I needed to hear it. At night, I would have vivid and memorable dreams that led me to chronicling a dream journal on a nightly basis and researching the symbolism the next morning.

Interestingly, without prompting, my coaching clients eventually even opened up about the synchronistic experiences which led them to start working with me in the first place. All this only compounded my belief in an intelligent force at work beyond my wildest comprehension—and working on myself allowed me to get there.

Practice 5: Experiment

"Very little is needed to make a happy life. It is all within yourself, in your way of thinking."
— Marcus Aurelius, Roman emperor (161–180 AD)

Over the past twenty-five years, I've encountered various stages of my spiritual growth journey: novelty, learning, excitement, going through the motions, loss of motivation, inability to see results, unconscious routines, grief, awakening and realization, back to learning, excitement, and conscious implementation.

The cycle ebbs and flows through peaks and troughs. In mid-2020, after my mom passed on, I experienced a shift within my consciousness. It took me out of the familiar material world I knew so well and placed me into a completely new one, where spiritual science was at the forefront.

When I chose to make spiritual growth and self-realization the North Star of my life, I started experimenting by combining techniques and modalities I had learned to create tangible actions that would carry me forward. I infused my logical, analytical, and scientific left brain with my spiritual, intuitive, and creative right brain. I would experiment by adding and removing things to my morning routine as an active way to test what would bring the deepest feelings of peace and focused accomplishment in my day-to-day life.

Some of the variables included the below, among so many other permutations and possibilities.

- What I said to myself the second I woke up in the morning
- The length and various techniques of my morning meditation
- Lighting candles or incense
- Pulling oracle cards after my meditation
- Drinking caffeine or not
- The types, intensity, and frequency of my workouts
- Listening to audiobooks or music on my morning runs
- What and how much food I ate for breakfast
- Listening to specific sound frequencies or guided visualizations while in the shower or on the way to work
- Reading passages from spiritual books during breakfast
- What types of journaling practices I would do in the morning

I was on a mission for answers through experience, and nothing was going to get in my way. I was like the spiritual Tim Ferris.

Tim is known for his 4-Hour self-help book series. He experiments with his body and work life to find the most optimal and time-efficient ways to go about his day. On the other hand, I was experimenting with spiritual and mental practices to find how to achieve calmness, gratitude, the greatest sense of inner peace, high vibration energetic states, a balanced mentality, and love.

Happiness and inner peace are almost entirely an inside job. Attaining that state of inner peace is the gateway to even-minded balance in your life. It also shows you the very real ability you have to tap into the boundless energy, the universal life-force or, in Sanskrit, *pana* coursing through you.

If you take a cadaver and fill its lungs with air, it will not suddenly come to life. There is a more profound force at play that gives your body its full capacity to function at the behest of your free will.

Dr. Bruce Lipton, PhD, is a quantum cell biologist who has conducted research at Stanford University, Pennsylvania State University, and the University of Wisconsin School of Medicine. He believes that every individual cell in our body is conscious.[35] Dr. Lipton conducted research by cloning stem cells to find that cells respond to their environment in a conscious mutative way to self-create specific outcomes.

Moreover, Caroline Myss, renowned medical intuitive working alongside Harvard professor of neurology, Dr. Norman Shealy, MD, similarly believes that our biography becomes our biology. In her best-selling book, *Anatomy of the Spirit*, Myss emphasizes how emotional and spiritual stresses or diseases are the root cause of most physical illnesses.[36]

This all seemed to resonate with me from lived experience. Just a few years prior, I remember being unable to move off the floor of my studio apartment in Manhattan due to unceasing lower back pain. After experimenting with Dr. John Sarno's twelve phrases to think psychologically instead of physiologically, I saw my seven-year stint with pain vanish in the matter of a few months.

As my own personal spiritual journey and connection to my angels continued to evolve, I was led to learn reiki energy healing from two gifted reiki "godmothers" at MINKA in Brooklyn, New York.

All of these actions were me living in a different way than I had been used to, changing small daily routines to see what worked best, and experimenting with every part of my life to unlock my greatest potential. It involved pushing my comfort zone and taking conscious action.

For years, I was highly skeptical of anyone who used the words "manifestation," "abundance," "law of attraction," "synchronicity," or "energy healing." Magic was reserved for the performers I saw on *America's Got Talent* or Las Vegas theatre stages.

My entire life, my narrative was to work hard, grind it out, and then see the fruits of my labor. To me, anyone who thought those etheric methodologies actually worked were delusional and not willing to put in the actual physical effort.

But as the saying goes, don't knock it till you try it.

I decided to research, learn, and implement hundreds of different techniques across meditations, energy tools, visualizations, breathwork, plant medicines, astrological and numerological lessons, psychological repatternings, journaling practices, angelic blessings, and personal development techniques on myself over nearly three years. While it's still ongoing every day of my life, what I came to find was that I could actually influence the events happening externally through my own self-management.

I started to see how some of the concepts of manifestation and attraction worked by first tapping into my own quantum field and reprogramming my own belief systems. By doing something different and experimenting with my life practices, I was able to create a simple, streamlined, and highly effective personal and spiritual growth practice in just five minutes a day. In the next section, I'll explain my Five Pillars of Greater Fulfillment.

It all still takes action. I haven't seen millions of dollars materialize out of nowhere or a six pack show up overnight—after all, "attraction" contains "action" within it. However, I started to see the power of tapping into the energetic blueprints of the physical world. I was able to cultivate a greater sense of belief, trust, peace, and surrender. Spirituality became a superpower.

As with everything, balance is the key—balance of directed action and intrinsic faith and belief that the outcome, or something better, is unfolding for you. I balance the benefits of meditation and journaling with constructive action and putting myself in motion to show the Universe that I am conscious of how I use my innate creative power.

In the spirit of life being a science experiment, my challenge to you is to try something different tomorrow. Take any small step to see how you can optimize your life in the best way for you. Maybe it works, maybe it doesn't, but that's what experimentation is all about. Follow the steps below with any practice you currently have or want to start implementing. In the below example, I use meditation, but you can do this with anything in your life.

1. **Ask yourself a question.** What happens if I meditate?
2. **Do your background research.** What are the benefits of meditation? How do I meditate? Where and when should I meditate?
3. **Conduct a hypothesis.** If I meditate, I will be calmer and more peaceful.
4. **Experiment to test your hypothesis.** Meditate for X minutes every day.

5. **Analyze your data and draw a conclusion.** What did I observe? Was I calmer? Was I able to handle situations more peacefully?

6. **Create a theory or retest.** This worked well and my hypothesis was confirmed, so I'll continue to do it. Or change a variable (place, time, duration, etc.) and retest.

Part 2:
The 5 Pillars of Greater Fulfillment

"Happiness is when what you think, what you say, and what you do are in harmony."

— Mahatma Gandhi, civil rights leader

The five-minute journaling technique for greater fulfillment has five core pillars to it.

What started out as a simple gratitude, release, and affirmation practice evolved into a multifaceted mindfulness technique that was rocket fuel for my personal growth journey. Let's dissect each of these five areas to understand how and why they work. Once you have the understanding behind them, you will be motivated to put them into daily practice in your own life. Through this distilled reflective technique, you will fast-track your way to profound states of inner peace, calmness, and vibrant energy.

Pillar 1: Gratitude

"Gratitude is a sacred space where you allow and know that a force greater than your ego is always at work and always available."
— Dr. Wayne Dyer, author and motivational speaker

What would it do for you to believe that every change that came into your life was beneficial for you?

Gratitude has become the overplayed song on the radio that you've heard every day for the past year and a half. You felt it all deeply in the beginning and reveled in its impact, enjoyment, and novelty, but soon it wore off. Life continued on, new songs were released, and new life situations came up that needed your attention. Over time, even though you knew the lyrics by heart, the song lost its shiny luster. It would come on the radio again, but you'd change the station because it was played out and too familiar.

I feel that the same thing has happened with the true and genuine appreciation of what gratitude has to offer in our daily life and modern society. Life today moves so fast, especially at work. Sincere thank-yous have been replaced with a three-letter "thx." Sometimes it even has connotations of passive-aggressive disapproval—that the work should have been done differently the first time.

Gratitude is often so overplayed that we forget to appreciate its simple yet profound impact. We are always told to be thankful and grateful. We practice thanksgiving with our friends and family every year ritualistically, but how much is it really internalized?

At Goldman, I lost count of how many times I was forwarded emails with no context asking me to inevitably do hours-to-days' worth of work. I was looped into email chains with my boss saying that I would handle a task ASAP. I never had a problem with this because I knew it was part of the job and culture. However, over the years, the lack of gratitude or appreciation that accompanied these requests began to crack my tough outer shell.

In open conversations with my friends at work, I started to notice that the other corporate hustlers I was surrounded by also craved this gratitude from the people they worked with. Receiving gratitude means you're being valued, recognized, and validated for your efforts. As human beings, we naturally gravitate toward a tribal and communal connection. As such, gratitude means that those people you're surrounded by see you. It gives you a deeper sense of meaning and connection—at work and in your personal life.

One way to create that connection is to give others what you desire, which is gratitude. It almost feels too easy, too simplistic, and too Golden Rule-y. However, countless scientific studies, like those done at University of California Berkeley,[37] have shown the benefits of gratitude. If you can show gratitude and empathy to others for the things they are able to bring to the table (regardless of how small), it lifts them up and in turn makes you feel happier by association. Looking at this through an energetic lens, it becomes even more clear why that is.

Gratitude is one of the building blocks of higher energetic vibration. You are acting in an appreciative and caring manner, which releases high-vibrational frequencies closely correlated to those seen in acceptance (350 on the Hawkins Scale—see Introduction) and love consciousness (500 on the Hawkins Scale). In resonating at this level, the energy field of the other person becomes charged and entangled with these energies, lifting them up. When viewing the relationship holistically, the energy between you and the other person is collectively amplified. It becomes a positive feedback loop that starts from within and grows. Gandhi famously said, "Be the change you want to see in the world."[38] This is an example of how that actually happens on an energetic level.

What you appreciate appreciates. Buddha told his followers that whatever they choose to give their attention to will amplify.[39] Where attention goes, energy flows. By focusing on the bright, beautiful, and good in your life, you will begin to see more of that because you are telling your brain what you want to focus on. Similarly, if you look for criticism, judgment, and dismay, those same feelings and patterns will boomerang back to you.

Michael Beckwith is a visionary author and spiritual director of the Agape International Spiritual Center in Beverly Hills, California. He explains this concept in an easy-to-relate-to way regarding twentieth-century parenting and childrearing. Growing up, you may have heard some parents say, "If you don't stop crying, I'm going to give you something to cry about." Beckwith attests that the Universal Law works in a similar fashion as it relates to gratitude: "If you don't stop being grateful, I'm going to give you something to be grateful about."

Gratitude is a synchronicity supercharger. It does this because it allows you to approach life, people, work, and circumstances from the heart. Gratitude allows your heart-center aperture to remain open as you move throughout the world. Gratitude allows you to learn, evolve, grow, and make progress in every situation. When you consciously and regularly practice gratitude in the now, it keeps you grounded in the present and always leads you toward your highest good and wisdom.

As I would find myself getting triggered by ungrateful bosses in the last few years of my banking gig, I started to implement a couple of gratitude and perspective practices at work. The first was *gratitude in the now*. When I would find myself getting angry at the way someone was communicating, treating me, or dumping work on me, I allowed myself the space to first acknowledge that it was making me angry and then approach it from a different perspective — one of gratitude for it.

I wrote a sticky note and put it on my monitor that reminded me to do this. It read, "I am grateful for everything happening in my life right now, especially the 'busy' and 'annoying.' Thank you for helping me grow." Every time I would find myself getting triggered by something, I would first bring awareness to the emotion so it could be seen. Then, I'd pull myself back into a centered state of gratitude.

Occasionally, I would even allow myself to visualize the person who was upsetting me as a close family member. I would treat them with the compassion and love that I would my dad or sister, even in times of disagreement. I interestingly found that using this technique sometimes would allow me to feel happier and at peace within myself, even if they didn't reciprocate the compassion back to me.

Gratitude roots you into the present and shifts your focus to what is immediately happening in the moment and around you. It's a recognition and appreciation of how much you are already a part of. When things feel overwhelming or that they're not going your way, it pulls you back to center and grounding. It shows you how much you've accomplished and the beauty of everything that is already yours. Gratitude can even work to fill you up with emotional joy in any circumstance and provide that boost of motivational lift to propel you forward.

Noticing repeating angel numbers or other signs from my mom on the Other Side is a reminder for me to practice regular gratitude throughout the day. Every time I see an angel number, I stop for a brief moment, close my eyes, even for a blink, and consciously think or say, "thank you." Doing this amplifies my gratitude practice and keeps gratitude for everything in my life top of mind. It also has the beneficial corollary of always improving my mood, due to the serotonin and oxytocin that's released as a result of practicing gratitude.

Pythagoras was a Greek philosopher and mathematician from the sixth century BCE who formulated the Pythagorean theorem and is considered to be the Father of Numerology. Pythagoras said that everything in the Universe is mathematically precise and that each number has its own vibration and meaning.

As you know, I use the numbers as a method of communication. Communication with my mom on the Other Side, and other angels/spirit guides who direct my life path. Showing gratitude for the ability to still feel my mom's presence and release into that trust is the least I can do. Gratitude and sentient recognition of the signs

I receive have interestingly opened new avenues of communication with my angel guides, to where I am now able to channel their messages for myself and others. I have also experienced greater and increased synchronicity in my life as a result (meeting new people, having unexpected/new experiences come my way, having business opportunities or clients led into my life, moving homes).

Practicing gratitude can also become a self-fueled goal. It's so easy to execute that you can lose everything and still be able to hit this goal of providing yourself the experience of being grateful for at least one thing every day (a healthy body, a cognizant mind, a chance to chase your dreams or rebuild, the opportunity to meditate).

This is why gratitude is such a fundamental pillar for greater fulfillment in life, and why the daily journaling practice first starts with three things that you are grateful for. It can be things in your personal life, physical appearance, family, relationship, job, or any number of things. There is nothing too big or too small to be grateful for. Ken Honda, prolific Japanese entrepreneur and author on finance and personal development, sums it up best. He says, "It comes down to a choice. Do you want to focus on hardships in the world or do you want to focus on seeing the world as a loving place?"[40] This is the gateway that gratitude opens for you. A gateway from which abundance, attraction, resonance, and manifestation are brought to you seemingly effortlessly.

Take a moment to pause and think about it now: What are three things you're grateful for?

Pillar 2: Letting
Go & Emotional Clarity

"Every new beginning comes from some other beginning's end."
— Semisonic, Closing Time

Inner peace can be hard to find on a Wall Street trading floor. Put yourself in my former banker shoes for a second. You are sitting shoulder-to-shoulder among dozens of rows of desks that span the length of one full city block. Phones are ringing nonstop throughout the day while bond salespeople yell across rows to the traders to sell hundreds of millions of dollars' worth of corporate bonds for their clients. The energy is high. One person's stress or disgruntlement can spill over into another person's headspace completely unconsciously. Before you know it, you're surrounded by expletives, judgments, projections of other's emotions and feelings, and tense energies.

It's not always a bad thing though. When someone executes a big block trade or a team successfully syndicates a loan or bond deal, the euphoria and intense joyful energy replicate that of a playoff sports game.

When life is flying by and every email you send out gets seen by hundreds of thousands of people on Bloomberg, you have no time to think about calmness or inner peace. Every character typed, every formatted table, and every mathematical calculation entered needed to be 100% accurate, down to three decimal points.

Before I started integrating conscious meditation or journaling practices into my everyday life, I would find myself drained and depleted by the end of the day. After an intra-day deal I worked on, priced, and allocated by 4 p.m., I would then start on all of the work I didn't have the time to get to during my nonstop day. On the subway or car ride home, I would pop in my headphones and whisk myself away on a sound journey to decompress. By the time I would get home nearing midnight, I would immediately pack my bags for the next morning, brush my teeth, and go to bed.

As my time at Goldman Sachs wore on, my own spiritual journey continued to deepen. I read philosophical teachings from spiritual thinkers around the world, like Paramahansa Yogananada, Sadhguru, Eckhart Tolle, Dr. Joe Dispenza, Pema Chödrön, Michael Singer, Brian Weiss, Marianne Williamson, and Don Miguel Ruiz to name a few. I also experienced my own spiritual channelings and downloads during ayahuasca and other plant medicine ceremonies in Peru, fire forgiveness ceremonies in Jordan, and breathwork sessions and meditations in New York.

One of the corollaries I drew through all of the teachings and experiences I've learned from is the need to release and let go. I've seen many people come to me with an inability to move past blockages based on previously lived experiences or setbacks, and this is completely understandable. Whether it's at work or in your personal life, if you experience a difficult setback, your brain and ego only want to protect you from a similar instance happening again in the future. It also thinks it's doing you a favor by predicting what is going to happen further on down the line, based on those previously lived experiences.

An example of this is making an error on a client presentation and having the fear of making a similar error again at the next client meeting. While it's important to learn from mistakes, this often results in excess anxiety, self-pressure, and premeditated fear—mental overbalance. This can also take the form of getting rejected by someone you like, consequently lowering your self-esteem, and discouraging you from approaching someone the next time.

I started consciously releasing and letting go of emotions, situations, or mindsets that I felt were commanding unnecessary use of my energy. First, I evaluate if that belief or feeling is still useful. If it's taking up unnecessary energetic space, I would then write it down to acknowledge and release it. I do this three times every morning for things I am letting go of. This then allows me to go about my day with lighter energy. It enables me to clear energetic and mental space of the things no longer serving me and allows me to achieve greater inner peace in the process. As a result, my thought power is then used for the necessary tasks I have in the present moment.

By understanding what those experiences were that created the belief and then delving into the feelings they incite, you are able to identify old patterns of thinking so that they can be released and replaced. These beliefs become the lens through which you drink in the world and can either make it a loving place of abundance and benevolence or a fearful place of lack, scarcity, and competition.

An awesome byproduct of letting go of things no longer serving you is that you also get more in-tune with your self-talk. This is the voice continually turning on the record player of your mind. When you then start to see that you are not those thoughts and that you can influence which beliefs you want to instill in yourself, you open the gateway to emotional clarity and expertise.

Release creates tangible separation from your emotions holding you back, and the resulting thoughts that lead to anxiety or overwhelm. Unblocking these emotions then allows your energy to flow freely up and down throughout your body and the various energy centers (chakras). Letting go of those beliefs or emotions once they're accepted helps you to become less reactive in your day-to-day life. You begin to spot what they are and how you tend to react to them. Thus, you're able to approach them from a space of compassion, acceptance, and release. Even when phones are ringing off the hook and your attention is being called in ten different directions, your ability to control your emotions through release is your ability to achieve inner peace in every situation you encounter.

Emotions should be viewed as data meant to be decoded. Emotions respond to stimuli and in turn generate feelings, which either cause you to act on the stimuli or not. Emotions can come in varying degrees of intensity ranging from a soft state (low) to a mood state (medium) to an intense state (high). Karla McLaren M. Ed, explains in her book *The Art of Empathy* that all emotions in the soft state can be beneficial.[41]

For example, anger can help you maintain your sense of self. A question to ask when you feel anger is, "What do I need?"

Apathy can mask anger when you cannot be openly angry. A decoding question to ask is, "what am I feeling?"

Fear helps you orient to change. A question to ask can be, "What am I sensing?"

Anxiety can help you organize yourself. A question to ask could be, "What does my step-by-step plan look like?"

Envy can help you to sense challenges that may destabilize your connection to security, resources, or recognition. A possible question for this could be, "What would be fair?"

Each emotion you feel is an opportunity to decode it and get to the root of why you feel a certain way. In doing this, the charge of the emotion begins to dissipate, and you choose the best path forward for you, which doesn't solely rely on an emotional reaction.

Releasing the Big 4

Over time, I've come to realize that consciously releasing four recurring aspects in my life have paved the way for grounded presence, spiritual awareness, and love for those around me. Every morning, I will write down and tell myself out loud what I am consciously letting go of. This helps me to create the necessary internal space I need to receive all that the day has to offer me—across all my various energetic bodies. The four aspects I recurringly found over years of release have been the letting go of judgments (of others), expectations (of outcomes), material desires, and attachments (to material things or to outcomes).

By releasing these aspects from my life, I have found that I am able to be more clear-headed and move through my days with ease and grace. Even if the day has some difficult tasks to show me, I'm able to handle them from a place of inner calmness and determination as opposed to frantic reactionary overwhelm and intense anxiety. At its core, the essence is to understand that all conditions, emotions, and states of mind are temporary.

Judgments

Judgments are part of life. Sometimes you have to make judgments in order to make progress. Do you take the train or drive? Do you go out to the party or stay in? Do you commit billions of dollars of Goldman Sachs's capital to underwrite the deal or not? These are all judgments—but they're ones that are helpful and imperative to moving forward in your life and career. However, it's when you make superficial personal judgments of others that you run the risk of falling back into unconscious awareness.

Often, you can find examples of this when the voice in your head judges others as you walk down the street. "Their pants are so out of style," "It sucks that he's bald at such a young age," "They should really go to the gym," "His voice is so high pitched," "She walks like she's full of herself."

Take a second to pause and listen to the ego voice in your head for a second. It is constantly judging situations, people, circumstances, and even yourself. Right now, it's probably judging the words on this page as well for bringing that voice into the light. The mental chatter can be unceasing for most people. It starts up first thing in the morning and sometimes doesn't even let you fall asleep at night for hours. By letting this voice continue to judge the things around you that don't move you forward, you are elevating and validating it. You are giving it the power over your true nature, which is inclusive oneness and acceptance.

The judgments I refer to releasing are those primarily associated with judging other people for non-constructive things. Sure, consciously judge a used car salesperson or new business partner to intuitively get their vibe. However, when you find yourself judging others with unconscious or unnecessary bias, bring awareness to this part of you and see what it is really trying to achieve.

In 1976, Helen Schucman and William Thetford, professors of medical psychology at Columbia University, scribed and published a book titled *A Course in Miracles*. The channeled book talks about a number of ways to regain your spiritual sight and belief in that oneness, but it also touches upon the unification of individuals and the reflective nature of our encounters and relationships.

What we choose to give to others and the world is what we receive in return. Radical separation runs rampant today. Separation across political parties, races, cultures, religions, nationalities, sexual orientations, and the list can go on and on in our world of duality. Yet among all the separation, there have been incessant calls for unification and collaboration throughout the centuries, from Mahatma Gandhi to Martin Luther King Jr.

If you dig deep into their words and ideologies, the root of what they are conveying is an inclusive acceptance of all. This is because all are inherently one. All are human. All are here for a reason, and all are valued equally. We are all fundamentally created of the same atoms, chemicals, and stardust.

Neale Donald Walsch, prolific spiritual author, phrased it best using the analogy of the human hand. He said, "If we understood that as a collective, we have decided to experience and express ourselves as merely individual elements of the same single thing. Even as the fingers of my hand are individual elements of the hand itself, which in turn is an individual expression of my body, and so forth. If all of the human beings, or every member of the human race saw themselves in that way, I promise you our collective experience would change dramatically."[42]

Life is a reflection of your internal states of being. Caroline Myss, in her book *Anatomy of the Spirit*, explains that the person you unconsciously judge (for intellect, appearance, demeanor) serves as the teacher for the inner healing work that you need to do. Concentrating on or judging the person will not heal you. You are only sent more teachers, each one more intense than the last. It comes down to learning the lesson from the teacher, not resenting or judging them. When you blame or judge a specific person, your ego is trying to protect you from shadow sides of yourself, which are yet to be integrated into your being. Judgment in this way is effectively and unconsciously slipping you into lower energetic vibrational states of fear and shame, completely unbeknownst to you. In judging the other person, you are leaking energy and giving your power away to your ego self.[43]

Within radical acceptance of the self, judgment begins to fall away. Once you start to see everything through the lens of universal oneness, you allow your heart to remain open to experiencing profound states of connection and joy as a result of loving acceptance for others.

Expectations

My guru's guru, Swami Sri Yukteswar Giri, lived in India from 1855 until his passing in 1936. In his teachings, he is quoted as saying, "I do not expect anything from others, so their actions cannot be in opposition to wishes of mine."[44]

Think about a time you were upset. Most of these times, you're upset because you didn't get what you want or expected you would get. Maybe you didn't win the business from a client you expected to, your highly anticipated dinner at a new restaurant was worse than you expected, your date didn't look as you expected from their pictures, or your friends didn't show up for you when you expected them to. The common denominator of the vast majority of these feelings of discontent are tied to your expectations of the specific outcome you desired.

Expectations aren't evil. They help you orient your goals, determine what is worth investing your energy into, and ultimately hold you accountable. However, the focus on expectations and more specifically, attachments to the outcomes of those expectations are what is keeping you from experiencing true inner tranquility and living life the way you want to.

My friend's father was traveling through India a number of years ago when a man said to him, "Expectations are just premeditated resentments."

Now this might feel extreme, but there is a deeper meaning to this. By releasing your expectations of specific outcomes, you are able to reduce the variability of emotional triggers. You open yourself to a new level of trust and benevolence of life and, in turn, a more centered state of consistent calmness.

Michael A. Singer's book *The Surrender Experiment: My Journey into Life's Perfection* is a forty-year chronicle of how releasing expectations of the ego voice in your mind can lead you on the most incredible journey of your life. One that is abundant, joyful, peaceful, and expansive beyond your wildest imagination. One that is meant for your highest good and wisdom.

Releasing expectations allows the flow of life to come in and flow *through* you—ultimately leading you to exactly where you need to be, when you need to be there. At first it starts slowly. Releasing the fact that rain changed your picnic date, your client chose another competitor, you missed a connecting flight, and even the unending productivity you demand of yourself. Over time, building that well of faith helps you trust that as long as you're doing all that you can within your abilities, what is unfolding beyond your efforts is exactly what is meant for you. Releasing expectations allows you to trust this flow in its entirety.

The more expectations you have, the more fear you have of the situation not turning out the way you want it to. Maybe it's the date you're going on, the client presentation you're walking into, or healing the chronic injury you've had. That fear is what ultimately self-sabotages you because you are coming into the situation from a place of lack and scarcity. If everything is energy, and thoughts create electrical impulses in the brain, then feeding yourself negative thoughts becomes the energy you carry within you and around you. Do you want to be the person with the dark and stormy rain cloud over their head walking down the sidewalk, or the bright sunshine magnetizing smiles from passersby? That internal energy attracts the external situations and circumstances to validate those thoughts. When you think about worst-case scenarios constantly and those situations come to fruition, all you are left saying is, "I told you so." The reason you're left with those words is because you attracted that energy toward you—consciously or unconsciously through your expectations.

Material Desires

After my mom passed on, I saw that no money or material possessions got carried with her to the afterlife. The desire for the next shiny object, newest devices, cars, and clothes only keep you trapped in the capitalist and materialistic cycle we're so accustomed to.

There's a fine balance. Treat yourself and enjoy life while you're here, but be real about it and ask yourself if your happiness is derived from those material things. In today's world, it's easy to stay on the hamster wheel for the sake of seeking the next material thing to make you happy.

While working in banking, material desires kept me trapped in the delusion that when I get to the *next* thing I want, *then* I'll be happy. The next bonus cycle will make me happy; the next vacation, bigger apartment, or new watch is what would bring me the happiness I so deeply craved. But that just wasn't it.

For years, I saw my income increase and my lifestyle expenses commensurately go up. The things I bought would bring a temporary sense of enjoyment, but my emotional states would always revert back to some level around their original baseline. Constantly chasing the next shiny object outside of you for happiness and enjoyment is exhausting and never truly leaves you fulfilled. Enjoy the material aspects in life, but remove the incessant focus on them. They're temporal in nature, and the true joy and fulfillment is derived from within and spreads without.

Material Attachments

Things in this world are only temporary. Your body, your clothes, your car, your house, and even your partner. All things in this physical plane must one day come to an end. As such, when you are deeply attached to the material objects, people, and places all around you, you are entrenching yourself in the physical and losing sight of the eternal spiritual. The latter is where you can tap into your infinite potential.

I remember looking at my mom's body at a private family viewing in the funeral home the day before her cremation. I remember looking at it and saying to myself, "This is just her body. Her spirit is with me. I can feel it." It was in that moment I realized that being attached to physical presences of anything wasn't the true essence of reality. I felt her eternal soul and light with me even after its departure from her physical form.

Detaching from the incessant identification of the physical as the be-all end-all, you drop into the world of energy. Now, just like all the things mentioned before—material attachments can be healthy in balance. It can keep you motivated to take care of a child or earn money to support your family. However, attachment too far to this end is where things begin to erode.

All of the big four are intertwined, and attachments and expectations display that. The dissolution of intensive material attachments makes room for intuition and synchronicity to fill in the gaps of your life. You become the patient observer and let life provide you with exactly what you need to experience in that situation—regardless of if it is what you wanted or not. This is a state of nonattachment to the expectations of outcomes and material things. In this state, you foster tremendous amounts of relaxation into the flow of life.

What becomes available to you when you detach from the physical focus of the person in front of you and focus on their soul essence instead? What happens when you detach from the physical focus of money solely for the sake of earning and spending and tune into the energy behind giving and receiving it?

What happens if you commit yourself fully to the process while you are in it? You give it your absolute best, maintain your grounding and presence throughout that moment, and allow the anxiety in your heart to release, open, and let it flow through and out of you. This is the release of tightly held attachment. This is called being fully committed and totally unattached.

Emotional Clarity and Happiness in the Now

Sometimes doing less, letting go, and simply being is when things unfold for you the way they're supposed to. I remember that I thought writing endless blog posts was what was going to bring me the greatest visibility for my business to grow. As I published my articles on Medium (a blogging website), none of them really took off. I was so deeply attached to them gaining visibility that I was approaching what I was doing from a place of lack and want.

Interestingly, when I took a two-month break to travel, meet various friends, go to Burning Man, and attend conferences and breathwork retreats, an article I published months earlier ended up going viral. No new posts were published in that time period, yet I received thousands of views, dozens of new subscribers to my newsletter, and throngs of new followers for my writing.

When you detach from needing the next thing to make you happy, you find the inner peace and happiness you crave is already with you in that exact moment—the paradox of intention. In Sandra Anne Taylor's book, *Quantum Success: The Astounding Science of Wealth and Happiness*, she explains that you must have goals, but your happiness shouldn't be tied to them. You must be happy before you attain them.[45] Interestingly, but probably not surprisingly, this disposition is what magnetizes your dreams, desires, and manifestations to you in an even more rapid manner.

If you believe you will only be happy when x, y, or z happens, you will never truly be happy. Those are just the physical symptoms providing momentary bursts of happy chemicals in the brain. They are fleeting and leave you chasing more.

Situations in your life are constantly evolving and you will always be running after the next thing to make you happy. Poet Adam Roa sat down with coach Peter Crone in a discussion about learning to truly love yourself. In this conversation, they touched on the subject of consistently chasing something you've never had. For example, if you are saying to yourself that you'll be happy when you have a wife, two kids, your dream house, and two luxury cars, you are probably not evaluating the full picture of what having those things entails. Given you've never had those things, you don't actually know if they will truly make you happy.[46] Thus, focusing on what you do have (through the lens of gratitude and nonattachment) is the gateway to lasting happiness, inner peace, and genuine success.

Medical intuitive Caroline Myss sums this up beautifully. Detachment does not mean ceasing to care, but rather quieting the voice of fear and fear-based decisions. She goes on to explain that the inner posture of detachment results in a sense of self that is so complete, external influences have no authority within your consciousness.[47] This is the true embodiment of wisdom. By focusing on maintaining your own states of inner peace and joy in the now, without tying it to attachments or expectations of future outcomes, you break through the walls of time and find the meaning of presence.

Release and letting go is also a tip of the hat to the impermanence of life. Pema Chödrön is an American Tibetan Buddhist author and disciple of Chögyam Trungpa Rinpoche. In her book, *When Things Fall Apart*, she talks about letting the impermanence of life intensify its preciousness. She explains that impermanence is a principle of harmony. When you don't struggle against it, you are in harmony with reality. This is exactly what the celebration of your birthday is. It's a celebration of the impermanent nature of your existence.

In this same vein, the release and letting go of emotions helps you maintain your inner states of harmony and peace. In the midst of an eighty-hour work week and back-to-back all-nighters, every little bit of emotional and mental capacity you clear up makes a world of difference. You are less easily triggered and on edge, less irritable, and although your body may be tired beyond belief, you are calmer and more emotionally stable. The best part is, it only takes one minute to feel into it and let it go.

Emotions are scientifically impermanent as it is. Brain scientist Jill Bolte Taylor explains that when you react to something in your environment, the neurological chemical process lasts for ninety seconds. Any emotional response thereafter is you choosing to stay in that emotional loop.[48] When you consciously choose to let it go, you are facilitating the process of releasing yourself from that emotional loop. As a result, you are clearing your energetic field to make you more capable and freer as you move about your life.

Obviously not all situations can *feel* like the emotion is only lasting for ninety seconds. Some situations carry intense emotional charge with them. In those situations, as with all others, it's always important to fully process your emotions first and foremost. Do not bypass them. Identify, then acknowledge and accept them. Use that data to then bring you from the mood or intense state down into the soft state of emotion. From there, you are able to let go and bring gratitude in. Doing so, no matter how difficult the situation may seem, is leaning into it and helping you grow in tremendous ways.

Psychologist Alyson Stone describes feelings as ocean waves. She says, "They rise, crest and recede, all day long."[49] If you let your emotions dictate your immediate actions, you are running through life in a short-sighted sprint of putting out fires. Not to mention, some of your emotional knee-jerk reactions will likely conflict with how you truly feel once the intensity subsides.

Everything is energy, and energy doesn't lie. When you can begin to understand and clear your emotions, new ways of perceiving the world, making decisions, and releasing anxiety into trust become available to you.

Close your eyes and feel into your heart, the largest electromagnetic field in the human body. What emotions or feelings feel stuck or trapped there? It might be from last night or last year. Identify it, feel it, thank it, and release it.

Pillar 3: Affirmations & Reprogramming Your Subconscious Mind

"Until you make the unconscious conscious, it will direct your life and you will call it fate."

— Carl Jung, founder of analytical psychology

"I love you. You are safe. You are whole. You are worthy. You are complete."

These are the words I wrote down on a sicky note and put next to my sink. Every morning as I would grab a glass of water, it was my reminder to put two fingers over my heart and say those five sentences.

I was at one of my lowest points in my life in November 2020, just a few months after my mom's passing. The person who loved me more than I loved myself was suddenly gone. I knew self-love was an area I needed to unlock for myself, but I hadn't started work with my own life coach yet. After a weekend of stargazing at Cherry Springs State Park in rural Pennsylvania, my friend Daniela suggested I start my days by saying these five sentences to myself. She told me if I did it regularly, I would start to change my outlook.

I felt like I was at the bottom of the bottom. I was in no position to judge how silly I would feel or look. I was willing to try anything.

Every morning, day after day, I would say these words to myself. I closed my eyes, concentrated my will deeply into the point between my eyebrows, and said the words with meaningful intention and fervor. Days turned into weeks, and weeks turned into months. Every morning, I would imprint those words with fiery feeling into my subconscious and superconscious mind.

During that timeframe, I started working with my life coach, and the effects began to snowball. Self-awareness went way up and distractions went down. I began to show myself love and rewire the negative self-talk driving my insecurities. No more fat-shaming myself or being overly critical about my body image. No more self-deprecating jokes at my own expense. No more telling myself I couldn't do something because of a poor excuse out of desiring comfort.

My vision for my ultimate desire in life became clear and specific. By the new year, I was focused on my spiritual, physical, intellectual, relational, and emotional goals. So much admiration and respect go to Dara, my first ever life coach, for opening my eyes to the endless possibilities already within me. She truly changed the course of my life.

Moreover, looking back on it all, it's interesting to see how just five sentences worked in the background of my mind for a couple months to set the groundwork for a belief system that continues to empower me.

The brain's role is to ultimately process information from your senses and respond appropriately by activating the necessary bodily responses and systems. One way to help the brain in this process is by telling your brain what you want it to focus on. The power of affirmations does just that. It begins to reprogram the subconscious mind and simultaneously create the intention and blueprint in the energetic realm using the superconscious mind.

The subconscious mind is the part of your consciousness that is not currently in focal awareness. It's able to be accessed if you focus deliberate attention and effort in its direction. Current scientific studies have now revealed that 95 percent of your life is created and governed by your subconscious mind.[50]

Picture an iceberg, for example. While some of the ice is visible above the ocean's surface, there is often a significant portion of ice below the surface. If the top 5–10 percent of the iceberg above the water is your conscious waking mind, the 90–95 percent below the surface is your subconscious and unconscious mind. This is what really operates you as you go about your day. Eating, breathing, digesting, memory formation—the way you react, feel, and believe the world is—all derive from your subconscious mind.

In the 1930s, Henry Ford, the founder of the Ford Motor Company, pushed his brightest engineers to believe in possibility. When Ford decided to produce his famous Ford V8 motor, he envisioned something that had never been done before. He sought to build the engine with the entire eight cylinders cast in one block. With this vision in mind, he instructed a small group of his most capable engineers to produce a design for the engine.[51] The design was drawn up, but some of the smartest mechanical engineering minds of the time stated that it was simply impossible to cast an eight-cylinder engine-block in one piece. Henry Ford replied, "Produce it anyway."[52]

In 1932, the Flathead V8 engine became a reality. As a result, he was able to keep manufacturing costs down, make the engine affordable to consumers, and drive the proliferation of his company's success. It is with this mindset that his quote "Whether you believe you can do a thing or not, you're right"[53] is truly embodied.

I was resistant to believing affirmations could have any real discernible impact on my life until I was actually forced to try them. After seeing the results and then understanding the science behind why it works, I rarely start a day without them. This is why affirmations are one of my Five Pillars of Greater Fulfillment.

To control your destiny (which is self-created, consciously or subconsciously), you must gain a perfect understanding of your subconscious mind—the mental faculty behind the conscious mind. The mind operates on memory and habits. Creation of habits depends on the length of time needed by the subconscious mind to create neuroplasticity (newly engrained networks) of experiences in the brain.

The subconscious mind is developed by meditation, affirmations, creative visualizations, artistic expression, exercise, and other techniques. It is up to the conscious mind to train the subconscious mind. While the conscious mind is the tutor of the subconscious, the subconscious can then act as the autopilot below the surface.

On the other hand, the superconscious mind springs forth from a deeper spiritual perspective. It is the all-knowing power of the soul that perceives truth directly; this can be considered your intuition. It's that level of awareness that sees beyond material reality and taps into the energetic blueprint behind everything.

Affirmations also work on the superconscious mind if you do them with genuine intention and concentration, not mechanical automation or lack of true belief. They are able to be sent into this level of ether and begin to morph the energy behind all things into manifestation of your deepest self-belief.

The ancient Chinese philosopher Lao Tzu lived over 2,500 years ago. He is famously quoted as saying, "Watch your thoughts, they become your words; watch your words, they become your actions; watch your actions, they become your habits; watch your habits, they become your character; watch your character, it becomes your destiny."[54]

Watching your thoughts and words is a conscious act, but once you ingrain it deep enough with consistent action, you let the subconscious and superconscious lead you to the daily habits to achieve the material and spiritual success you desire most.

More recently, it's been discovered that the brain's reticular activating system (RAS), which is the link connecting the brain and spinal cord, plays a vital role in regulating consciousness, motivation, and perception. It filters inputs from the five senses and adjusts your overall level of mental alertness.[55] When you are able to able to tell your brain what to focus on, it will consciously seek out the results and answers to guide you.

Think about the classic road-trip game, "punch buggy, no punch-backs." When you're driving down the road and spot a Volkswagen (VW) Beetle, you playfully punch the person next to you. The other person, keen to reciprocate the jest, is now highly alert for VW Beetles. This is an example of your brain's RAS at play.

Intuition coach, Christie Marie Sheldon, talks about a new method of question-and-affirmation called lofty questions. It involves asking yourself an action-oriented question that affirms or manifests for yourself.

For example, if you want more money and abundance, instead of affirming, "I am financially abundant," try, "Why am I so financially abundant and have more than enough money to provide for myself, others, and my dream life?"

The common "I am" affirmation certainly has its benefits. It's empowering and ignites immediate self-belief. I still regularly use it, but it also has its drawbacks. Often times, when using the "I am" form of affirmation, the egoic voice in your head can want to counter that new belief you are trying to embed.

With lofty questions, you are asking a question that shows you believe you already are that. It also asks your brain's RAS to find the right cues to answer the question. Just like when you are focusing on finding the next VW Beetle on the highway. After practicing a lofty question for myself, I'll typically sit with it for a moment and answer why that lofty question is true. Once you start to do this, you begin to see the ways in which you already are the things you are affirming—further strengthening your magnetic field for that outcome.

Just as with the other pillars, affirmations and directing your brain's RAS also work to bring you into the right situations, relationships, and synchronicities to make it your reality.

Maybe you've seen the job requirements of being a "self-starter" listed on a job opening. Affirming belief in yourself not only reprograms your subconscious mind but develops greater levels of self-confidence, self-trust, and intrinsic motivation. The power of affirmations lies in its simplicity. Once you acknowledge the voice in your head telling you that you look silly, you kindly thank it and ask it to leave. From there, you are able to step into your miraculous power through conscious rewiring of your subconscious mind.

Close your eyes, put your right pointer and middle fingers over your heart, take a deep breath, and repeat these five sentences out loud three times: "I love you. You are safe. You are whole. You are worthy. You are complete."

How do you feel?

Pillar 4: Synchronicity

"There are no coincidences. We meet people intentionally who have been put on our path for a reason—sometimes sooner, sometimes later."

—Dr. Kenneth Harris, chiropractor, transformational teacher, and healer

In late July 2021, my sister and brother-in-law were celebrating the pending arrival of their new baby girl with a trip to Nantucket. They called me one day on their trip and shared a bizarre and unexpected story.

Earlier that day, they decided to change their plans and go to the beach in the morning to avoid the rain showers forecasted for the afternoon. After arriving at the beach, they were met with swarms of fellow beachgoers, all with the same idea of beating the rain. They pulled a last-minute change and diverted to a different beach. When they arrived, they found the new location was close to empty, and they happily set up their chairs.

As my sister and brother-in-law were relaxing and reading, they were suddenly approached by a couple who asked them to take their picture. As they began talking, the gentleman introduced himself as Dr. Ken Harris. He was celebrating his seventy-fifth birthday and mentioned to them that he and his wife, Judy, had taken a walk on Brant Point Beach for his birthday every year for the last fifty years.

The couple mentioned they lived in New Jersey, where my sister and I grew up. He took the opportunity regarding the mutual state of residence to explain that he had written a best-selling book on the topic of synchronicity.

As they talked further, they found that my sister, brother-in-law, and Dr. Harris were all physicians. So far there were a couple of likely overlaps but nothing out of the ordinary. That day, my sister was wearing my brother-in-law's Duke University hat. Dr. Harris remarked that he just got off the phone with a good friend whose son went to Duke and asked if my brother-in-law knew him. Interestingly enough, both my brother-in-law and the named student were in the same a cappella group.

Things were continuing to get interesting, so the conversation went on.

Dr. Harris noticed my sister was holding the book *The Autobiography of a Yogi* by Paramahansa Yogananda in her hands. She was rereading it for spiritual inspiration a year after my mom's passing and in preparation of becoming a mom herself. She asked if Dr. Harris happened to know the author, and he immediately responded that he did. He mentioned that for the past twenty-plus years when visiting his son in California, he would make a trip to visit Yogananda's SRF meditation gardens on the Encinitas coastline.

The spontaneous conversation continued, and they shared a number of other overlaps including stories of Dr. Harris hosting Indian priests at his house for healing work and my sister mentioning my new endeavors as a spiritual life coach.

When my sister recapped the full story to me on the phone, I was both stunned and elated. I immediately looked up his book (*Synchronicity: The Magic. The Mystery. The Meaning*), ordered it, and read it cover to cover in less than two days.

After reading Dr. Harris's stories of synchronicity, I was inspired. My sister meeting him that day on the beach seemed like far more than just random chance. This was the definition of synchronicity — the occurrence of events having no discernible causal connection, but highly relevant significant meaning.

A short while later, my sister connected us. We visited him in New Jersey to learn more about his life as a chiropractor in private practice and the holistic healing work he had been undertaking for the last forty-five years. Dr. Ken Harris cracked me open to the idea of synchronicity, and suddenly all of the signs I was receiving started to make sense.

These signs — the angel numbers, feathers, rainbows, messages written in chalk on the sidewalk, storefront signs, songs on shuffle, meditation insights, books I was told to read, courses and certifications I was guided to take, clients magically brought into my life — were all synchronicities in some way, shape, or form.

All of these circumstances were occurring more often than I could even imagine, and in countless ways beyond just noticing number patterns. This was no coincidence.

In the beginning, I didn't believe it. Maybe I didn't want to believe it. Was I just looking too deeply for meaning? But I decided to turn the volume down on that incessant egoic mental chatter and lean in.

Every day, I wrote down three pieces of synchronicity or things I noticed that felt like magic in my life. Over time, it became evident to me: there was something more happening. This was my mom communicating on the Other Side, but this was also something much grander. It would take an army of angels to send me this many signs.

The magic of synchronicity was swirling around my entire life. I started to tap into the symbolism behind everything I saw, not just numbers. Recurring themes in social media posts, the messages hidden in the subject lines of junk emails, meeting new friends who felt like long-lost connections, a friend's intuitive feeling about collaborating on business projects, pictures and books found in Airbnbs, seeing roses (one of my mom's signs) everywhere I went, the calm behavior of wild animals I encountered, drawing oracle cards of topics I was thinking about just a moment earlier, and feeling/seeing energy more profoundly and deeply every day.

Dr. Harris was the missing piece that put it all together. The more I wrote down and noticed these signs hidden in plain sight, the more new ones showed up in my life. The synchronistic messages continued on. Books and articles of things I needed to read to answer questions on my mind were given or presented to me seemingly out of nowhere. Friends in Argentina would think of me right before I texted them. Five unrelated people across various parts of my life would say the same recurring word to me in a two-day span. I received intuitive insights with my reiki energy clients during healing sessions, and they would then validate them. Eventually, others' loved ones who had crossed over also started appearing to me with messages for them.

However, my favorite of all forms of synchronistic messages and experiences has been the meeting of new people. Mentors, guides, business partners, and friends all started to come into my life. People I'd never met before started opening up to me and asking for help without even knowing I was a life coach. The cashier at a grocery store expressed her sudden urge to tell me about the passing of her husband. Cab drivers from New York to Cairo would start talking to me about their life story and struggles. A chance connection with someone in Los Angeles led to experiencing invite-only breathwork sessions in New York. It was utterly fascinating.

Reflecting on all of it, I gained a core takeaway of why synchronicity is so incredible. It is accessing the true spiritual power within you through the power of presence. In slowing down to be absolutely at one with the moment around you, you are able to notice the small things, which can have large and meaningful impacts in your life. It allows you to do less by stepping into greater trust, following your intuition, and releasing your fear-driven narratives. The latter of which—fear—is most commonly the subconscious motivating factor for the vast majority of decisions you make in your life.

Synchronicity is a sign of flow. It means you are in coherence with your heart and mind, balanced with the greater energetic frequencies of the world around you. In this state, you live relaxed and at ease while still moving forward. A state of peaceful progress.

In August 2021, I was intuitively called to join a masterclass on quantum mechanics hosted by Sky Nelson-Isaacs, a physicist, author, and professor in California. I saw him speak briefly in a docuseries I watched, but I didn't know much about him other than that. He started by explaining quantum mechanics as the study of what the world is doing when you are not watching it. As the talk went on, he explained Bell's theorem. It states that whenever two subatomic particles interact, they never forget that association and so remain energetically entangled no matter how far apart they might be — quantum entanglement.

Nearly half a century earlier, Swiss psychologist Carl Jung coined the term *collective unconscious*.[56] The collective unconscious, occasionally called the objective psyche, refers to the idea that a segment of the deepest unconscious mind is genetically inherited, instinctual, and not shaped by personal experience. In essence, Jung believed there is a level of unconsciousness shared across all people that was inherited from the past collective experiences of humanity.[57]

Coupling John Bell's scientific theorem with Carl Jung's psychological view of the collective unconscious, you can deduce that synchronicity is the evidence of the interconnected nature of life and our human experience.

Nelson-Isaacs went on to explain that in life, you are moving along a timeline between touchpoints; life is not coming at you. He shared his fence-post model of time, where in between the fence posts of goals and aspirations you have for major life events, there is an open space of pure potentiality. The connection between any two posts does not necessarily need to be linear. It is within this open space that synchronicity evolves to bring you one event or another, based on the felt experience and mindset that is attracting you to different branches linking the two fence posts.

Life feels more fun and lighthearted when synchronicity is involved. It can also only truly be appreciated in its magnanimous glory when you slow down. Instead of swimming up against the rapids of a flowing river, you are guided along its stream with ease and peace. When you slow down, you grow in a way that reduces the friction and resistance of the seemingly incessant needs of life.

In 1827, German physicist Georg Ohm made a discovery about electrical circuits that is dubbed Ohm's Law. He found that the amount of current in an electrical circuit is inversely proportional to the resistance in the circuit.[58] Said differently, the more resistance there is, the less energy can flow.

When you are caught in a perpetual cycle of jumping from one task to the next, mechanically going through your day, or in a frantic, reactionary, or overwhelmed state constantly, you are building up resistance in your body.

This resistance often takes the form of burnout, apathy, anxiety, fear, stress, anger, worry, apprehension, or overthinking. That emotional and mental resistance then prevents you from living an energetically aligned life with the inner and outer success you seek.

Slowing down doesn't always need to mean stopping or doing less. Rather, it means being more deliberate and intentional. Being intentional means doing something with purpose. It means being strong and determined in action toward accomplishing that purpose.

What happens when the reason you do something is no longer tied to *needing* the specific outcome? The task no longer becomes a means to an end but rather the end itself. Your intention is fully focused on the task at hand. You know that if you put in your absolute best in that moment, that is all that can be asked of you, and the chips may fall as they may from there.

· With a clear conscience, you have knowingly committed yourself to the cause. In doing so, you are following the very principal Zen teachers have been preaching for ages. Embodiment of each task and the present moment in its infinite entirety.

However, in order to be consciously present, you have to discipline your own thoughts to not have other thoughts dominate or take over in that moment (Practice 2). This restraint takes you out of your head so you are not consumed by incessant internal chatter. Meditation works to train you how to do this (Practice 3).

Is it a coincidence that the moon is exactly the same size as the sun in the sky? The moon is 400 times closer to Earth than the sun, and 1/400th of the diameter. This allows for a total solar eclipse.

Perhaps, but if you begin to be present in every moment, you will notice the magic and synchronicity happening everywhere around you. Guiding and directing you to exactly where you need to be. Just like the other pillars, synchronicity amplifies the more you are aware of it and treat it with the appreciation it deserves.

So, what is one synchronicity you noticed today?

Pillar 5: Manifestation

"My method is different. I do not rush into actual work. When I get an idea I start at once building it up in my imagination. I change the construction, make improvements, and operate the device entirely in my mind."

— Nikola Tesla, inventor and engineer

Since my middle school days, I always knew I wanted to work in finance and be an investment banker (as shown by Bakshi Bucks) even beyond seeing my mom work in healthcare finance. And on some level, there was a cultural/societal norm expecting me to go into a professional field like medicine, law, finance, or tech.

At the time, the point of life in my eyes was to be successful. That meant making money, having status, and providing for loved ones. My parents emigrated to the United States with the American Dream in mind, and if I could continue to achieve their legacy, I would.

I never knew much about manifestation, nor did I believe it was possible. All I knew was that if I worked hard and gave it my all, I could achieve my goals.

Even as little as three years ago, I thought the concepts of manifestation and attraction were the biggest bag of bologna and waste of time one could ever spend their precious energy on.

People with their head in the clouds could talk about manifestation and abundance all they wanted, but down on Earth, I knew that hard work and my own personal effort is what actually drove real results.

However, when I received the inspiration in those first three months of 2021 to begin a new chapter of life in service to others, I wanted to learn and start making an impact quickly. I put out the specific intention, but I still wanted to expedite my timeline so I could build my business as soon as possible.

During that phase, I stumbled upon a number of teachers, websites, and videos explaining various techniques of manifestation. I began to follow them closely for weeks and months. It was during this same time period that life coaching certifications, business coaches, new clients, mentors, and collaborators started pouring into my life. The things that I needed to complete my vision were literally materializing before my eyes in a matter of months and in unexpected ways (thank you, synchronicity).

Knowing what I know now, I can't help but smile as I look back on my journey of becoming an investment banker. I can genuinely say that I manifested the dream job and life I envisioned as a twelve-year-old. I put out the conscious intent to be an investment banker, and through my vision, action, effort, and belief, I reaped the fruits of that manifestation. But what if things could happen faster now that I'm more aware of how to use the energy of manifestation?

In my years studying techniques of manifestation, attraction, quantum potential, and abundance mindsets from greats like Bob Proctor, Michael Beckwith, Dr. Joe Dispenza, and Gabby Bernstein,

I've come to realize my own personal take on manifestation—and it can be boiled down into a simple equation.

Manifestation = Intention + Resonance + Action + Detachment of the Specific Outcome

Intention is the determination that keeps you aligned with your purpose and action. Understanding your why is a crucial aspect of deriving commitment for your intention.

Resonance is all about vibrating at the frequency of that which you wish to become. To visualize resonance, record yourself plucking each string on an acoustic guitar. Then, place the guitar on top of the speaker and play back the recording. You will notice that each string on the guitar will vibrate at the exact time it is played on the speaker. This is resonance at work, and it operates with your beliefs, ideas, thoughts, and actions just as it does the strings of a guitar.

When you resonate at a specific frequency of energetic vibration, you are putting out that energy into the world. Like the resonance of a guitar, that energetic vibration will come back to you in the people and circumstances you encounter.

In manifestation, this is the concept of the Law of Resonance. Some people like to call it "fake it till you make it," but when you are consciously aware of what you're doing, there's no faking it. You know that the future you who has manifested their dreams and desires is already out there, and you are just resonating at the vibrational energy and mindset which that future you embodies. Empowerment through embodiment.

This is where things like affirmations fuel the intrinsic self-belief to help you reprogram your subconscious mind to believe it. It's already out there, you already are that, you're just magnetizing it toward you through the Law of Resonance. It is also crucial to infuse this resonance with gratitude that it has already happened. Ralph Waldo Emerson, the American philosopher and writer who led the transcendentalist movement of the mid-nineteenth century said, "Once you make a decision, the universe conspires to make it happen."[59]

Action is self-explanatory. Your manifestations don't work unless you do. You need to do your part to put out your creative energy and effort. With patience and firm resolve, you will reap the fruits of your labor, or you'll be led on a path where something even better unfolds. This is where detachment comes in.

Detachment from the expectations of specific outcomes is what allows synchronicity and flow to lead you to where you need to be. It opens the portal to your pure creative consciousness. Here, you are fully committed and totally unattached. You are present and working toward the inspiration that flows through you, trusting that benefits will be realized in due course and as they are meant to. It is knowing that while the intention is out there for what you desire, the Universe may have even grander plans for you. This is why releasing the specific outcome can allow for something better to potentially enter your life.

Through this equation, manifestation comes into form in your life. The alpha state of brainwave activity, guided creative visualizations, and various energy merging techniques can expedite your realizations of this, but there are also simple techniques you can put into practice right now.

In August 2021, I was focused on manifesting my first three full-paying coaching clients by the end of the month. Every morning, I took out a small notebook that was my manifestation journal and followed a simple practice.

1. In a notebook, write down what you want to manifest in a present-tense sentence — as if it has already happened (and infuse gratitude into it).

2. Write the same sentence down the page five to fifteen times. However many will comfortably fit on the page without going overboard.

3. After it's written down, close your eyes, smile, and say the sentence out loud to yourself the number of times you wrote it down. Take a deep breath between each sentence, and with true intention and feeling, believe that it is already yours. It helps if you focus your attention as if you are looking at the point between your eyebrows (the third-eye or pineal gland) and visualize your manifestation vividly.

4. Truly *feel* what it's like to already have that manifestation in your life as you say it. This is important, because it allows your body to feel the emotion of already knowing that energy, thereby pulling and magnetizing that vibration toward you.

5. Most importantly, see two or more people benefiting from your manifestation. This amplifies the effect and allows you to live in congruence with your genuine heart space. It is a symbol that you are creating not just for yourself, but for

the benevolence of humanity. We are here to help raise and elevate each other up—physically, emotionally, mentally, and spiritually—and seeing others benefit alongside you is in alignment with that understanding.

6. Go about your day with the feeling that what you are manifesting has already happened.

7. Repeat this daily. Release the "wanting" aspect, which comes from a place of lack, and embody the already "knowing" feeling, which comes from a place of abundance.

I did this daily that August, telling myself that I have three full-paying clients by the end of the month. As the month began, I received one client in the first week and another in the middle of the month. Yet by the last day of the month, I still only had two clients. I had been practicing my technique daily, but it just hadn't worked. That last day of the month, I received an inbound email from someone who wanted to set up a discovery call. The earliest she could speak was the next morning, so we set up the call and spoke. As we wrapped up the call, she told me she didn't need any time to think about the decision and was immediately all-in.

This story of manifestation blew my mind. It actually worked to bring me the exact number of paying clients in the timeframe as I envisioned. My last client did contact me by the end of that month. I did notice, though, that at the time, I wasn't totally detached from the specific outcome. I was growing my business and wanted to expand and grow rapidly, so I was quite invested in the result.

While it worked that time, it also led me to seeing some things I was manifesting not come to fruition. For various reasons, I either wasn't fully committed, or the specific things I was trying to manifest just weren't meant for me at that time. This is where your why and use of your intuition comes in. Sometimes it makes sense to continue pushing toward your goals if you truly intuitively feel that it is meant for you and you're not just coming from a place of wanting for superficial reasons.

If something isn't meant for your specific path of growth, the doors will close, and sometimes it is to be trusted. Continuing to run up against the doors and bashing them in can eventually get you what you want, but it's often more strenuous, feels harder, and can be coupled with things you didn't want alongside it. It's life's way of gently nudging you toward what's in your Highest Wisdom, even if you don't realize it at the time.

When you surrender, life isn't meant to be hard. Yes, there are learning and growing lessons. Yes, there are trials, difficulties, and painstaking grief. Yes, some days and months will feel harder than others. But when it continually feels like you're swimming against whitewater rapids every day and every year, there is a broader energetic imbalance in your life that needs to be addressed.

My entire life, I thought the only tool I had was hard work. I might not have been the smartest kid in my grade by pure academic standards, but I always knew that putting in the extra work would pay off—and it often did. From office hours with professors to weekends in the library and asking my friends to tutor me, I did my best to excel as far as I could.

Now I'm not saying there's a substitute for hard work, because there really isn't. At least not one that I've found yet. However, there are countless additional tools you can tap into through the power of spirituality and understanding how the energy of the world around you operates. Even growing up in a spiritual family, I never really knew the true power that spirituality could help me unleash in my life. It took living through life lessons over decades for me to finally come to terms with my own personal desire to go deep into spirituality with conscious intention.

One tool that has changed my life is the Most Benevolent Outcome (MBO). Tom Moore, in his book, *The Gentle Way: A Self-Help Guide for Those Who Believe in Angels*, explains how to request MBOs from your angels and spirit guides that allow you to go about your day in a less stressful and more gentle way.[60]

Benevolence is doing something well-meaning with a warm heart and pure intention. When you ask your angels for MBOs, what they will do will only be done if it is benevolent for you and all others. They can never encroach on your or any others' free will and will only act when called upon for something you want to happen—not something you *don't* want to happen or to another's detriment.

MBOs can be requested for anything in your life. From finding a parking space, to the most cost and time effective way home. I've requested MBOs for dates, business meetings, physical healing, emotional well-being, and productivity. It's important to remember that *most benevolent* doesn't always mean easiest. For example, if you request an MBO for the best parking space for your car, this may not be the one closest to the store. The one closest to the store may have someone back out and hit your car, whereas one a few spaces down might have some money still left in the meter and leave your car collision-free.

After reading Tom Moore's book, I experimented with MBOs in everyday life, and the results only proved to deepen my well of faith. They've been one of the greatest manifestation and higher guidance tools I implement in every situation I need. I've shown this to complete spiritual nonbelievers, and after witnessing the power of MBOs from their guides over a couple of weeks, they now use this practice on a daily basis and tell others about it.

I now request an MBO with the intention of how I want my entire day to go from my morning meditation to falling asleep at night. There are nuances and specific ways to go about it for different requests and magnification of outcomes, but the gist follows a basic script.

"Angels and energetic beings of love and light, I request a Most Benevolent Outcome for _____. Thank you."

I've probably requested thousands of MBOs so far in my life, and they have always worked in my favor. What I've noticed is that whether they come to fruition the way I believe they will or not, my highest good is always supported and I can feel that shift. It removes the incessant need to focus on and worry about the future outcomes in life. It allows you to live fully in the present moment, knowing that your angels and guides are working to allow the most benevolent outcomes in your life to unfold regardless of what happens. When I request MBOs, I meet my guides halfway with my own intentions and efforts, the rest of what will unfold is for my Highest Wisdom, whether I realize it in that moment or three weeks later.

I can't emphasize enough that all of these practices—whether gratitude, affirmations, or MBOs—must be done with complete belief, feeling, and faith. Going through the motions won't help you or anyone else. The spark needs to come from the deepest parts of your soul with conscious intention.

It's like a basketball coach and their team. The coach can draw up the plays, help the players condition themselves for game time, practice, train, challenge them past their limits, and motivate them on gameday. However, the desire to achieve is self-driven by the players and that's when the real impact is realized.

The conscious intention needs to come from within for the spark to ignite through action. From there, hard work no longer becomes the only tool in the toolbox. Manifestation, intuition, gratitude, letting go, MBOs, energy healing, breathwork, affirmations, and so many other spiritual tools become available to you to use alongside the inevitable action and effort you need to undertake.

This is why life coaching holds such a special place in my heart. The spark comes from within you. Then I as the coach provide the tools, techniques, questions, and frameworks to help you achieve your goals.

Looking back at a reflection I wrote in my journal on December 29, 2020, I'm amazed at how fruitfully my vision has evolved in just a couple short years. The excerpt read:

> "My ultimate desire for my life is to live an honest, fun, and emotionally and spiritually fulfilling life. To achieve material success that allows me to provide an even better life for my family, and more importantly to attain a very deep sense of inner peace and spiritual understanding that I can pass down. I want to give back and help others materially where possible, but ultimately want to be someone who people turn to for advice, guidance, wisdom, and spiritual awakening. I want to help people unlock success in the physical and spiritual dualities of life."

At the time, I was still in the thick of things at Goldman Sachs. Life coaching was nowhere on my radar, and I hadn't even begun to receive messages in my morning meditations yet. I put out the intention into the Universe, and detaching from the outcome, that intention began to expand and magnetize the people and circumstances meant to help me achieve that vision. Without even knowing it, I put into action another manifestation for my dream life. One that I already see the fruits of every single day.

Now it's your turn. Take a second to think about the dream life you envision for yourself. Close your eyes and allow yourself to dream big. Bring in all of the sights, sounds, tastes, smells, and feelings associated with you in that dream life. See others benefiting, express profound gratitude, and allow your cells to resonate at that frequency and feeling.

Five Pillars of Greater Fulfillment — Daily Journaling Practice

"This one page a day will change your life."

—Neal Bakshi

When I first started on my personal growth journey, gratitude was the doorway from which the remaining four pillars of my daily practice evolved.

As I went deeper into personal development, I started to supplement this with a five-minute daily journaling practice during breakfast. On a fresh page in my journal, I listed three things I was grateful for, three things I was consciously letting go of, and three things I was affirming for myself (including in the form of a lofty question).

The results were pretty amazing. In the matter of a couple months of regularly doing this, I noticed a dramatic shift in the way I showed up at work every day. I was happier, more present, calmer, less restless, less stressed, and more confident in my abilities at work, with clients, and in my personal life. If it sounds too good to be true, it's not. My friends in and out of work could notice a shift in my energy, and I frequently received feedback on it. It got to the point where they would ask what changed and I would share my simple journaling exercise.

When I gave a talk about finding greater fulfillment to a group of analysts, associates, and vice presidents at Goldman Sachs before I left the firm, I shared this tangible practice with them. After receiving their feedback, they were excited about it and started to incorporate it in their schedules.

Yet while I was doing this, I was still keeping a separate journal for the things I was manifesting in my life and a notes list on my phone for the synchronicities I noticed during my day. As an investment banker glued to my computer screen, every task I performed needed to be highly efficient. As such, my personal development practice was starting to take up more of my precious time and resulted in task-switching, which would take me out of flow states at work.

Time is precious in the fast-moving life of a corporate hustler. Ultimately, after over a year and a half of experimenting to see what worked best, I found a way to streamline my personal growth practice. In less than five minutes a day (meditation not included), I could open my heart, release emotional baggage, foster inner strength, drop into alert presence, and manifest my deepest desires.

As a result, my Five Pillars of Greater Fulfillment were formed, and I couldn't imagine my days without it. The efficacy lies within its simplicity, intention, and your own belief.

The Five Pillars are (1) gratitude, (2) letting go and emotional clarity, (3) reprograming the subconscious mind (affirmations), (4) synchronicity and magic, and (5) manifestation. After utilizing these five simple keys of life as a daily part of my morning routine, I can feel the energetic shift within me. Beyond that, people I meet for the first time repeatedly tell me, "I love your energy" — a compliment I'd never really heard before.

It all sounds great in theory and concept, but the proof is in the real-world results that come from implementing this practice in your life.

You will find your emotional state feeling lighter, happier, and more loving in all of your day-to-day interactions.

You will feel like you are growing and making progress each and every day.

You will feel less moody or swayed by your emotions and thoughts.

You will be able to separate from your thoughts and get out of your own head.

You will release trapped feelings within your body to allow your energy to flow more freely.

You will be less reactive and find levels of peace you never knew existed within you.

You will start to reprogram the 95 percent of your brain that subconsciously drives your life and cultivate incredible self-confidence, self-belief, and self-trust like never before.

You will pick up on the synchronicities and messages of guidance happening all around you in every moment.

You will be able to speed up to get more accomplished, while simultaneously slowing down and feeling relaxed and at ease during the process.

Your mind will feel clear and focused, while you are also able to tap into your intuitive guidance to lead you on the right path without any guesswork needed.

Throughout it all, you will find ways to magnetize your dreams into your life and create the life you genuinely want to live and feel fulfilled with.

So how can you integrate these Five Pillars into a simple less-than-five-minute technique to get the greatest transformation as quickly as possible?

Easy—with just one piece of paper and a pen every day, you can completely unleash and rewire your full energetic potential, and expand your perspectives in the process.

Below is what the template looks like for the daily pages. You can also head over to https://www.nealbakshi.com/bankingonangels and download a free journal to get you started.

[Date]
Grateful For:

1. _____
2. _____
3. _____

Letting Go:

1. _____
2. _____
3. _____

Affirmations:

1. _____
2. _____
3. _____

Magic (Synchronicity):

1. _____
2. _____
3. _____

Manifest:

1. _____
2. _____
3. _____

A completed example is below:

8/4/22
Grateful For:

1. Being healthy and safe as I went about my day yesterday.
2. The signs of guidance (and angel numbers) I receive everywhere.
3. My daily journaling and writing practice.

Letting Go:

1. Judgments or jealousies about other people.
2. Worry about the awkward joke I made at dinner and what they think.

3. Material attachments and desires keeping me glued to the physical world.

Affirmations:

1. Why does financial abundance flow with ease into my life from everywhere?
2. I am worthy.
3. Why am I so seamlessly in the flow of life?

Magic (Synchronicity):

1. Seeing angel number 555 on the clock in the morning and evening and on a license plate and building number.
2. Walking into a random store to get something for a friend and finding the perfect birthday present for another friend.
3. Driving past graffiti of an octopus five seconds after Jen was talking about the octopus art car at Burning Man.

Manifest:

1. I am grateful to be an international best-selling published author.
2. I am grateful my business is helping to serve the world and grows with ease.
3. All of the perfect clients are magnetized to me, and I am grateful that I can help them for their Highest Wisdom.

As you can see, it is incredibly straightforward. If you practice this one-page exercise consistently every day, you will find greater balance in your daily life. You will go about your day with a much clearer mind. You won't find yourself overthinking as much and getting stuck in thought spirals, which take you out of the moment.

You will feel lighter and happier with all of your interactions. Your confidence and sense of self will dramatically improve, and others won't be able to help but notice.

This practice makes personal and spiritual growth easy, mindful, and fun. Just like working out, once you start to see the results, it becomes intoxicating and exciting. This one-page exercise brings the often ethereal and intangible concepts of spiritual growth into a concrete practice that you can use to unleash the limitless power within you. Try it out and personally feel the inner and outer energy shift in your life. This is the road to true and lasting success.

Part 3:
Living with Angels

Now that you know the techniques to implement in your life and why they work, the next step is bringing this high-vibrational energy with you throughout your day. Tools to tap into your intuition, cultivate consistency, and keep energetic balance top of mind will all work toward helping you stay aligned with the Universe and on track toward your goals.

Intuition

"Intuition is a very powerful thing, more powerful than intellect, in my opinion. That's had a big impact on my work."
— Steve Jobs, founder and CEO of Apple Inc.

If the founder of the first trillion-dollar company is touting intuition, there's got to be more to it than just spiritual happenstance.

Once you are able to open your heart (gratitude), release (let go), cultivate self-belief (affirmations), and be present (meditation and noticing synchronicity), you are well on your way to having expertise over your emotional and mental states. You are no longer reacting to the external stimuli but are in-tune with the deepest part of your energetic being. This is where your intuition shines through.

Intuition is the ability to understand something immediately without the need for conscious reasoning. It is that immediate "gut feeling" you get—and it is not limited to a certain group of people. Everyone has the ability to tap into it, but often life is so noisy, you can't discern the difference between your intuition and your racing thoughts unless you're in an emergency situation.

There are a few ways to cultivate intuition, but they all start with quieting the noise around you and within you. From there, you can actually hear and feel the voice of your intuition.

Intelligent intuition is a process I've cultivated for myself with the help of monastics and spiritual teachers. As oxymoronic as it sounds, there's a method to the madness—and from personal experience, it works.

Simply put, it's the ability to . . .

1. Focus on your breathing and come into a place of silence and stillness
2. Quiet the mind and let thoughts subside
3. Quiet the heart and let emotions subside
4. Come back to a place of centeredness and use your willpower to hold this space
5. Once you feel a vibration of virtuous harmony and coherence, call up the question in a broad or general manner
6. Hold the space and let the question rest within your calm and centered space
7. Feel with your heart and listen to any guidance directing you
8. Come back to your breath, smile, and open your eyes with gratitude
9. Now use both your faculties of intelligent and logical discernment (left brain) intertwined with the intuitive "gut feelings" and felt-senses you received (right brain) to come to an intelligent, intuitively-derived decision. The left-brain aspect should help you see the physical action steps needed to manifest that heart-led guidance into form.

Try this practice now with anything you need to decide on in your life.

Consistency Is Key

"It does not matter how slowly you go, as long as you do not stop."
—Confucius, Chinese philosopher (551–479 BCE)

Starting something new is one of the most interesting feelings. Excitement about the prospects of positive change intersects with the trepidation you feel about the road ahead. You're energized, motivated, have a big vision, and are driven beyond belief. Simultaneously, you're stepping into something you've never done before. Fears, doubts, insecurities, procrastination, and uncertainties can all come out of the woodwork to sabotage your new endeavors.

I always come back to a visual I learned about a classic double-pan balance scale. On one side of the scale is your belief and faith in attaining the goal you set out to reach. The other side is all of the fears and doubts you have about being able to actually reach that goal.

Pick a vision you have and take a look at the scale through your personal perspective. If the scale is at 20% belief and 80% doubt, you are fighting an uphill battle against your own mind. Even if it's at 50% belief and 50% doubt, you are still pushing an incredible amount of counterweight against your own ambitions. The fear and doubt may never totally subside, but your mindset is one of the most powerful variables you can control.

To really drive your goals home, you need to have the intrinsic faith and belief of your outcome at 90% and reduce the fear factor down to 10%. There's always a level of preparedness and evaluation of the situation holistically; but oftentimes the biggest thing holding you back from achieving what you truly desire is yourself. If Henry Ford barely believed a single-block V8 motor could be created, his engineers would likely have not had the drive to do the previously unthinkable.

Mindset may sound like a life coaching motivational tactic, and it certainly is, but even psychologists like Carol Dweck, PhD, author of *Mindset: The New Psychology of Success*, attests to the importance of having a growth mindset in all you approach. When you fundamentally believe change is possible and that you are not just a one-dimensional fixed being with your innate skills, you are on the right track. There may be setbacks along the way, but your mindset is what will help you to learn, grow, evolve, and adapt to the circumstances.

If a baby attempted to take its first steps but fell down while doing so, you wouldn't see a parent give up and say, "Well, I guess my kid can't walk." On the contrary, you would see that parent continue to encourage the child until they were able to take those steps on their own. The same thing could be said when you attempted to do multiplication or division for the first time. If you got the answer wrong, you didn't just give up and assume you would never learn it—you kept going, learning, course-correcting, and trying until you figured it out.

Small changes over long periods of time equal big results.

In February 2022, I was at the Private Placement industry conference for my job at Goldman Sachs. Every year, bankers, investors, lawyers, and rating agencies in the structured finance world descended upon Miami for a weeklong conference to talk business, industry trends, and hot button topics. We set up individual meetings with all of our investor clients, but one meeting particularly stuck out to me.

In the meeting, one of the largest investors we work with told us that they deployed a record $1.1 billion dollars for their program in 2021. They were able to invest in bonds, which allowed them to hit their return targets, portfolio diversification needs, and deploy an all-time record of cash for the year. I thought about this for a minute and came to an important realization. If they invested money for a day, they wouldn't come close to investing $1.1 billion. If they invested money for a week or even a month, they likely would still not be close to breaking their all-time record. If they even invested for half a year, chances are slim they would hit their target, let alone surpass it. It took them a full year working to diligently underwrite deals and ultimately invest their record $1.1 billion in privately placed bonds. They stayed the course and saw the results of their effort.

This story is analogous to your own personal growth and development. If you start a meditation or journaling practice like the Five Pillars, you likely won't see any results in just a day. If you did it a few days a week for a month, you are still not being consistent enough to make a meaningful impact in your mindset or in your life. Within a few months, you are likely to see some progress, but it may not be at a highly noticeable level. However, if just like our investor client, you consciously implement the journaling practice on a daily basis, you will look back on your year and see leaps and bounds of incredible growth.

If you continue this or other personal development techniques over three, five, or even ten years, you're looking at a completely different life than the one you're in right now. Take the example of simple versus compound interest in a savings account. You can continue to earn the same amount of interest on your principal as in simple interest; or over a long-term horizon, you can earn interest on your principal plus any other accumulated interest, as in compound interest. This accumulated interest is the equivalent of your personal development work. Over time, you will gain greater self-awareness, go deeper into your own psyche, and connect smaller pieces of the puzzle over long periods of time to see profound wisdom and spiritual growth emerge.

It feels like just yesterday I started the journey with my mom as one of my guardian angels. However, it also feels like it's been ongoing for countless years. What started as numbers evolved into words and eventually angel card channelings for me and others. I voraciously learned the things I was guided toward and worked on practicing them daily in my life. Consistency is the key to anything. From my mom and my own spiritual journey, the greatest lesson I've learned is to keep on keepin' on.

It may seem daunting to look at a new situation. You may want to procrastinate or turn your head away because you don't know where to start. But if you can see the first step in front of you that you need to take, just focus on that and take it.

In anything you've worked toward in life, the underlying variable you used to get you to where you are now is consistent action. Motivational speaker Zig Ziglar once said, "Repetition is the mother of learning, the father of action, which makes it the architect of accomplishment."[61] You didn't make it to where you are in your career overnight. It took years of education, learning, working, and growing to look back and see where you are today. The same holds true for personal and spiritual growth. It's a journey that you need to make progress toward in any way you can every single day.

One question that helps me move forward is asking myself, "What is the one thing I'm committed to completing today?"

Some days it can be a big task like finishing a pitch deck or Excel model, writing a chapter of a book, or executing a full bond deal in a day. Other days, it can be as simple as taking the dog for a walk, doing laundry, or spending time to reflect and journal. Life ebbs and flows, but as long as you are doing something on a daily basis that is moving forward with intention, you are building your habit of consistency.

Everything Is Energy — Balance Leads to Lasting Success

"Learn how to see. Realize everything connects to everything else."
—Leonardo da Vinci, Italian polymath

Energy pervades everything around you. Electrical signals fire in your brain's synapses every time you think a thought. You expend energy as you go about your day moving and working. You eat food to give you more energy, and you recharge your battery at night during sleep. Energy comes from the Greek word *energeia*, which means "activity or operation." It stems from the word *energos*— quite literally, meaning "in" (en) "work" (ergos).[62]

Any activity or operation you perform—be it moving around the world physically, feeling emotions that release countless hormones or activate neurotransmitters in the body, thinking, meditating, or even breathing—is an expression of energy.

In today's unceasing and overstimulating world of energy, balance doesn't just show up at your doorstep. It involves conscious intention and energy management. Ancient Chinese philosopher Lao Tzu talks about The Middle Way as a path for finding balance in life.

The example is based on the Buddha who spent years going to extremes from riches to asceticism to find the meaning of life. Eventually, he heard a music teacher explain to his pupil that if he tuned his instrument too tight the strings would break; too loose and the instrument would not play properly. This is the essence of The Middle Way. As Lao Tzu expands upon in the Tao Te Ching, understanding that all external circumstances and mental states are temporary helps you avoid overreacting to any one situation.[63]

Aggregating your physical, emotional, mental, and spiritual existence, you arrive at a singular essence that makes you, you. The energetic balance in your life across these areas is what leads to profound realizations of inner peace and the real success of having complete dominion over yourself.

Science is just starting to explain what sages, gurus, and spiritual teachers from India to Greece have been alluding to for thousands of years. As part of this, doctors, scientists, mathematicians, physicists, and cosmologists are testing theories that shine a light on the true nature of human consciousness.

Through self-awareness, meditation, and techniques from my Five Pillars (gratitude, letting go, affirmations, synchronicity, and manifestation), you can start to use some of this new science to be at the forefront of the collective spiritual evolution of humanity.

Just as the benefits of yoga caught on like wildfire, it's only a matter of years before meditation, breathwork, energy healing, and other mindful modalities begin to transform the landscape of our cultural beliefs. We stand at the precipice. One that pushes the boundaries of what we previously thought was possible—as individuals and as a collective.

As I reflect back on what led to me following my interests in energy healing and life coaching, it all comes back to my greatest hero—my mom. I remember the last time we talked before her surgery. She called me a couple days prior, on my birthday.

The last words she ever said to me were, "Your mother's blessings are always with you." Little did she know that I'd replay those seven words in my head for years to follow.

They continue to give me strength and guidance. Through the situations that have unfolded for me in my life since, I know that her energy is still very strong and present in my life. She is the angel helping to orchestrate the concert of my life from above. It is her energy, which is lighting the lamps along my path and helping me to tune in to the synchronicities in life at every turn.

It's the energy that led this former investment banker on the path to help you realize your full potential and unlock lasting success—though the power of spirituality, inner peace, and energetic balance.

Next Steps

Now that you've learned tangible tools and techniques to find a greater sense of fulfillment, inner peace, and energetic balance, take advantage of these free resources at your fingertips. They will help you to continue your journey and amplify your progress.

Visit https://www.nealbakshi.com/bankingonangels for the full list of free resources to help you on your personal growth journey.

If you're interested in learning more about coaching and other ways to work with me, book a free thirty-minute intro call with me at https://calendly.com/nealbakshi/30min or by scanning the below QR code.

Stay connected on any of the social media platforms below!

 @neal.bakshi

 Neal Bakshi

 @nealbakshi

 @nealbakshi

Your Review Makes a BIG Difference

Congratulations and thank you for taking the time to read and finish my book! 😊

This book was guided into your hands for a reason. Nothing happens by chance. The fact you finished the book is a testament to your innate drive and willpower. You are someone who cares about personal growth and unleashing the full and balanced power of your energy.

I'm grateful you've trusted me to take you on this journey of knowledge and self-discovery.

My goal is to share practical wisdom, spiritual knowledge, and tangible techniques to allow you to live the most balanced, peaceful, and successful life you can dream of.

I appreciate your support, and it would mean the world to me if you took just a few minutes to leave an honest review of my book on Amazon or wherever you purchased it!

With your help and support, we can help countless others around the world cultivate inner peace and tap into the boundless world of energy all around us.

Thank you!
Neal

Acknowledgments

I want to send immense heart-felt gratitude to the people along my life path who have opened my mind, mentored, guided, taught, and assisted me in writing this book and leading me to where I am today.

First, to the gurus, sages, angels, and spiritual teachers from Self-Realization Fellowship and beyond who have shown me the way to find the light within myself.

My incredible family: my mom, Simi Bakshi; dad, Aneesh Bakshi; sister, Salina Bakshi; and brother-in-law, Vivek Upadhyay. Thank you for your endless support and counsel.

I thank my friends across my various phases of life, from childhood through adulthood, who have provided me endless laughs, shared experiences, and companionship.

I acknowledge the incredible efforts from my book writing coach, Jake Kelfer, for guiding me, motivating me, and holding me accountable. Thank you to the incredible Carly Catt for her help editing this book and to the rest of the design and formatting team.

Thank you to the mentors, colleagues, and friends at Goldman Sachs who have helped me learn and grow so much through their energy and support. I am eternally grateful for my years at the firm.

I especially acknowledge Dara Poznar, my first ever life coach who helped change my life; Leah Gervais, my good college friend and first business coach; Jonathan Quigg (Quiggy) for being a catalyst for my personal growth journey; and Dr. Ken Harris, for your mentorship.

I want to thank my clients—past, present, and future. I am grateful to have the opportunity to work with you and guide you along your path in this lifetime.

Thank you to *you*, the reader of this book. You are here for a reason.

Last, but certainly not least—thank you to all of those on the book launch team who helped make this possible in every respect.

Author Bio

Neal Bakshi is a certified spiritual life coach, reiki energy healer, and angel channeler. He specializes in guiding highly driven, motivated, and aspirational next-gen leaders achieve inner peace, lasting success, and energetic balance through the power of spirituality.

He is a former Goldman Sachs investment banker and left his vice president title to pursue his spiritual passions, including teaching meditation and breathwork.

Neal grew up in a spiritual family, meditating since he was five years old. He embodied his spiritual practices to live a peaceful and balanced life in the finance world and now helps others in the corporate and entrepreneurial world to do the same.

His vision is to bring the benefits of spirituality and personal growth into the mainstream by making spiritual teachings highly relatable with factual scientific backing and positive psychological approaches.

Endnotes

Introduction

1   We're all just walking each other home," Ram Dass according to Goodreads Quotes, accessed December 14, 2023, https://www.goodreads.com/quotes/40582-we-re-all-just-walking-each-other-home.

2   "Energy," Merriam-Webster.com Dictionary, Merriam-Webster, accessed December 1, 2022, https://www.merriam-webster.com/dictionary/energy.

3   "Conservation of energy," Wikipedia, accessed December 1, 2022, https://en.wikipedia.org/wiki/Conservation_of_energy.

4   Vishen Lakhiani, "The Code of the Extraordinary Mind," The Bregman Leadership Podcast, Episode 69, April 10, 2017, https://bregmanpartners.com/podcast/vishen-lakhiani-the-code-of-the-extraordinary-mind/.

5   Donald C. Chang, "A quantum interpretation of the physical basis of mass-energy equivalence," Modern Physics Letters B 34, no. 18 (2020), https://doi.org/10.1142/S0217984920300021.

6   Kerry D'Ambrogio, "Everything—Including the Human Body—Is Made of Energy," Massage Magazine, December 3, 2019, https://www.massagemag.com/energy-field-120110/.

7   Kerry D'Ambrogio, "Everything—Including the Human Body—Is Made of Energy," Massage Magazine, December 3, 2019, https://www.massagemag.com/energy-field-120110/; Dr. Joe Dispenza, Becoming Supernatural (Carlsbad, California: Hay House Inc., 2017).

8   "The Four Bodies," goop, written by Editors of goop, reviewed by Jill Willard, updated April 9, 2015, https://goop.com/wellness/spirituality/the-four-bodies/.

9   "What Is Proprioception?" WebMD, written by WebMD Editorial Contributors, reviewed by Dan Brennan, reviewed on November 27, 2021, https://www.webmd.com/brain/what-is-proprioception#:~:text=Proprioception%2C%20otherwise%20known%20as%20kinesthesia,thinking%20about%20your%20next%20step.

10   Daniela Rabellino, Paul A. Frewen, Margaret C. McKinnon, and Ruth A. Lanius, "Peripersonal Space and Bodily Self-Consciousness: Implications for Psychological Trauma-Related Disorders," Frontiers in Neuroscience (Dec 2020), https://doi.org/10.3389/fnins.2020.586605.

11   Karla McLaren, The Art of Empathy: A Complete Guide to Life's Most Essential Skill (Louisville, Colorado: Sounds True, 2013).

12   "The Four Bodies," goop.

13   Efthymios Tzounis, "Constructing and Deconstructing the Terminology of Spirituality: A Journey Back to the Greek Roots," J Tradit Med Clin Natur 6, no. 248 (2017), ISSN: 2573-4555

14   Rumi, according to Arjuna Ishaya, "Welcome the rub," Medium.com, November 24, 2020, https://medium.com/@arjunaishaya/welcome-the-rub-f0b15ec1ac36.

15   "Jeffrey Allen" website homepage, accessed December 1, 2022, https://www.iamjeffreyallen.com.

Part 1

16 Academy of Ideas, "Carl Jung on Overcoming Anxiety Disorders," YouTube, February 25, 2019, https://www.youtube.com/watch?v=CP1YOeNnZac&t=1s.

17 Carl Jung, Civilization in Transition, second ed. (London, UK: Routledge & Kegan Paul, 1964).

18   Peter Crone according to TeamSoul, "Peter Crone: This Is Why We Suffer (And This Is How We End Suffering)," Fearless Soul (website), December 2, 2020, https://iamfearlesssoul.com/peter-crone-this-is-why-we-suffer-and-this-is-how-we-end-suffering/

19 Jeffrey Allen, "Duality," online course, Mindvalley, accessed December 1, 2020, https://www.mindvalley.com/duality/?itm_source=storefront&itm_campaign=du_evergreen&otag=storefront_du_top_navigation.

20 "Autobiography of a Yogi: Last Gift of Steve Jobs," Yoganda Satsanga Society of India, July 18, 20114, https://yssofindia.org/blog/autobiography-of-a-yogi-last-gift-of-steve-jobs.

21 Michael A. Singer, The Untethered Soul: The Journey Beyond Yourself (Oakland, California: New Harbinger Publications/Noetic Books, 2007).

22 Singer, The Untethered Soul.

23 "Electroencephalogram," NHS, reviewed January 5, 2022, https://www.nhs.uk/conditions/electroencephalogram/#:~:text=An%20electroencephalogram%20(EEG)%20is%20a,looked%20at%20by%20a%20doctor.

24 "What Are Brainwaves?" brainworks (website), accessed December 1, 2022, https://brainworksneurotherapy.com/about/faq/what-are-brainwaves/.

25 Dawson Church, The Genie in Your Genes: Epigenetic Medicine and the New Biology of Intention (California, US: Energy Psychology Press, 2009).

26   Dawson Church, "Mystic Brain," online course, Mindvalley, accessed December 1, 2020, https://www.mindvalley.com/mystic-brain/.

27   Church, "Mystic Brain."

28   Church, "Mystic Brain."

29   Church, "Mystic Brain."

30   Amishi Jha, Peak Mind: Find Your Focus, Own Your Attention, Invest 12 Minutes a Day (San Francisco, CA: Harper One, 2021).

31   "The day Science met Spirituality," The Awakening Times, February 4, 2015, http://awakeningtimes.com/science-spirituality/.

32   Randy Alcorn, "Florence Chadwick and the Fog," Eternal Perspective Ministries, January 21, 2010, https://www.epm.org/resources/2010/Jan/21/florence-chadwick-and-fog/.

33   "Florence Chadwick," Wikipedia, accessed December 1, 2022, https://en.wikipedia.org/wiki/Florence_Chadwick.

34   "We can't solve problems by using the same kind of thinking we used when we created them," BrainyQuote, Albert Einstein, accessed December 1, 2022, https://www.brainyquote.com/quotes/albert_einstein_385842.

35   Russell Brand, "Your Cells Are Conscious!!! Awaken This Deep Power," YouTube, December 22, 2020, https://www.youtube.com/watch?v=6XmhVB8AIt0.

36   Caroline Myss, Anatomy of the Spirit: The Seven Stages of Power and Healing (New York City, NYC: Harmony, 1996).

Part 2

37   "The Science of Gratitude," white paper, Greater Good Science Center at UC Berkeley, May 2018, https://ggsc.berkeley.edu/images/uploads/GGSC-JTF_White_Paper-Gratitude-FINAL.pdf.

38   Arleen Lorrance, The Love Project (Brooklyn, NY: LP Publications, 1972).

39   Lynne Twist, "What You Appreciate Appreciates," chopra, August 7, 2014, https://chopra.com/articles/what-you-appreciate-appreciates

40   Ken Honda in article by Brigid Hackett, "Brainz: The #1 Key to Building Wealth with Ken Honda," kenhonda.com, February 22, 2021, https://kenhonda.com/brainz-the-1-key-to-building-wealth-with-ken-honda/.

41   Karla McLaren, The Art of Empathy: A Complete Guide to Life's Most Essential Skill (Louisville, Colorado: Sounds True, 2013).

42   Neale Donald Walsch, "Neale Donald Walsch on The God Within Us," Mindvalley podcast, podcast, March 20, 2018.

43   Myss, Anatomy of the Spirit.

44   Gita Krishna Raj, "Gods' divine gift—Guru," Pranava, printed in Frozen Thoughts, accessed December 1, 2022, https://sites.google.com/a/maverickfitness.net/pranava/Home-page/articles/gods-divine-gift--guru.

45   Sandra Anne Taylor, Quantum Success: The Astounding Science of Wealth and Happiness (Carlsbad, California: Hay House Inc, 2006).

46   The Deep Dive with Adam Roa, "Deep Dive #105 | Peter Crone—Learning to Truly Love Yourself," podcast, December 2019.

47   Myss, Anatomy of the Spirit.

48   Bryan E. Robinson, "The 90-Second Rule That Builds Self-Control," PsychologyToday, April 26, 2020, https://www.psychologytoday.com/us/blog/the-right-mindset/202004/the-90-second-rule-builds-self-control.

49   Steve Ferber, "How the 90-Second Rule Can Change Your Life," The Daniel Island News, October 14, 2020, http://thedanielislandnews.com/opinions/how-90-second-rule-can-change-your-life#:~:text="Feelings%20are%20like%20ocean%20waves,re%2Dstimulating%20our%20internal%20circuitry.

50 Olga Blias, "Your subconscious mind creates 95% of your life," Thrive Global, June 6, 2021, https://community.thriveglobal.com/your-subconscious-mind-creates-95-of-your-life/.

51 Henry Ford, "When Henry Ford decided to produce his famous V-8 motor, he chose to build . . ." Goodreads Quotes, accessed December 1, 2022, https://www.goodreads.com/quotes/257316-when-henry-ford-decided-to-produce-his-famous-v-8-motor#:~:text="When%20 Henry%20Ford%20decided%20to%20produce%20his%20 famous%20V%2D8,a%20design%20for%20the%20engine.

52 Bill McGuire, "The Ford V8: Henry Ford's final triumph," Autoweek. com, June 5, 2003, https://www.autoweek.com/news/a2098616/ford-v8-henry-fords-final-triumph/.

53 "Whether you believe you can do a thing or not, you are right," Henry Ford quotation in The Reader's Digest, September 1947.

54 "Watch your thoughts, they become your words; watch your words, they become your action . . ." Goodreads Quotes, Lao Tzu, accessed December 1, 2022, https://www.goodreads.com/quotes/8203490-watch-your-thoughts-they-become-your-words-watch-your-words.

55 "Your Brain at Work: The Reticular Activating System (RAS) and Your Goals & Behaviour," LifeXchange, accessed December 20, 2022, https://lifexchangesolutions.com/reticular-activating-system/.

56 "Collective unconscious," Wikipedia, accessed December 1, 2022, https://en.wikipedia.org/wiki/Collective_unconscious.

57 Lisa Fritscher, "What Is the Collective Unconscious?" VeryWellMind, updated March 18, 2022, https://www.verywellmind.com/what-is-the-collective-unconscious-2671571.

58 "Ohm's law," Britannica, updated November 21, 2022, https://www.britannica.com/science/Ohms-law.

59 "Once you make a decision, the universe conspires to make it happen," BrainyQuote, Ralph Waldo Emerson, December 1, 2022, https://www.brainyquote.com/quotes/ralph_waldo_emerson_383633.

60   Tom T. Moore, The Gentle Way: A Self-Help Guide for Those Who Believe in Angels (Flagstaff, Arizona: Light Technology Publishing, 2006).

Part 3

61   "Repetition is the mother of learning, the father of action, which makes it the architect of accomplishment," BookTrust, Zig Ziglar, accessed December 1, 2022, https://www.booktrust.org/blog/book-trust-key-three-key-3-consistency/repetition-is-the-mother-of-learning-the-father-of-action-which-makes-it-the-architect-of-accomplishment-zig-ziglar/.

62   "energy," Vocabulary.com, accessed December 1, 2022, https://www.vocabulary.com/dictionary/energy#:~:text=Energy%20is%20from%20Greek%20energeia,or%20light%20to%20do%20work.

63   "The Tao Te Ching: Verse Twenty-Three," Overcoming Caregiver Fatigue, MFW Consultants (website), May 6, 2012, https://mfwconsultants.com/the-tao-te-ching-verse-twenty-three/.

Made in the USA
Middletown, DE
23 January 2023

22898581R00104